The Misfits

MW01245274

By Robert J. Zito

Copyright © 2004 by Robert J. Zito

All rights reserved

ISBN: 1-4116-0709-0

Table of Contents

Dedication

I dedicate this book to Moe (short for Maureen), the love of my life. She was the first person to whisk away the curtain to see the real person who operates the controls of the almighty "BOZ."

Without her understanding and masterful editing skills, this book would not have been possible.

Technical & Historical Consultant

As I get older, the past is a faded memory of a story or movie I once read or watched. That is one reason this story needed telling. If not now, when?

I like to thank Mark (Starship) for helping me remember most of the details. I have known him for longest time and trust him the most. All of the technical and historical details that are correct are due to him. The mistakes I made on my own!

Disclaimer

Some of the stories herein are based on actual events. The names were changed and selected at random and the names chosen do not reflect actual people now living or that have moved on to the next phase. Some of the stories and events were slightly altered or fictionalized to prevent any possible repercussions.

Forward

Many of us had traumatic childhoods and some of us had, or are having traumatic adulthoods. We all have had feelings of sadness, loss, and loneliness at some time during our lives. I think this comes with being mortal and human. Sometimes the sadness just gets too much and we need someway of draining some of it off. Crying is one of nature's "safety valves" that helps drain off unbearable sorrow. One of the things we "learn" early about being male is we are not supposed to have these kinds of feelings. Men are supposed to "suck it up" and always be strong. Sayings like, "Be a man about it" or "Take it like a man," were some typical phrases bandied about when I was a child. Our family and society have taught us these types of emotions are weak, childish, or a feminine attribute. I do not feel that way. Men do have these feelings. These feelings are all part of the human condition.

I, being an almost properly indoctrinated male, hardly show a trace of emotion in my daily life. Not even the most socially accepted male emotions of anger or frustration. My emotions are under tight lock-down. If anything, I am told that I have a sullen, pensive look. I am different around the people who have penetrated some of my multilayered walls of protection.

My writing is different. My mind is unbounded. It is close to being a religious experience for me. It is a catharsis, which may come from the confessional for some, and the daily social interaction for others. It is an expression of self and creativity that is art for the kinds of people I can identify with. Writing is my art. At times, it has also been my confessor, confidante, and most intimate friend. I cannot betray it. It compels me.

I write from my feelings. All our experiences are colored by emotion. We cannot be an uninvolved bystander. If we stripped away all our emotions, we would become an inhuman machine capable of doing anything without remorse or emotional consequences. I don't think that this is possible for a human being. At least, it is my fervent hope that it is not possible!

There are many "truths" to a writer. I feel a novel can contain more truth than a documentary. What makes a novel more believable and grab you in a place deep inside? It's when you can feel the emotions and they agree with the inner truth you find inside. It is not the everyday truth like declaring you went to work or washed the car. It is the inner truth that resonates down to your secret self. All of us have secret selves. Some of us have more developed inner persons than others. In some, this inner person hides more than in others.

Some of us don't even realize we have them. Usually these people are always physically active. They schedule every minute of their day with either work or play ventures. They never have a free moment to sit back and reflect. Sometimes this is by design. I think they may fear what they might find lurking there. You and your therapist are the only ones who know for sure!

Our minds can be a scary thing especially if they have errant, uncontrollable thoughts that scare the shit out of you! How do you rein in a run-away mind? I sometimes feel mine should have an emergency red "cutoff" switch, like there used to be at the top of the steps that lead to basement, for the furnace. Every time you feel your mind is going out of control, "bam!" You throw the switch and now your mind is only capable of the rudimentary functionality necessary for day-to-day normal life. Some might suggest I shouldn't be able to reset it, so once I enter the normal mode so I could never get out!

The creative writer tries intentionally to expand the volume of "the box" we have been "taught" by experience we must stay within. He or she should strive to explore and enlarge the confines of their creativity. They should also try to keep at least one foot near the ground so they can feel around and see they can still touch it every once in a while!

I feel there should be a "get to know your mind day." The only reason it would be unpopular is you probably wouldn't buy a surprise present and a "Hallmark®" card for yourself to celebrate it! Oh well, if it isn't merchandisable, it will never happen!

When I write, I unleash my internal, feral animal and it kidnaps me and takes me on a wild, sometimes, painful ride.

This writing may seem melodramatic to some. It was written in the mind-set of an introverted teenager who didn't have any friends, close family or companions. Dealing with your teenage years in a normal environment is hard enough. Being perpetually on the outside looking in, in a world without the social skills needed to acquire acceptance, is traumatizing.

To those who read this and feel that it is not "right" for a male to feel this way, then I ask you to go on a journey through your own mind and at least be honest with yourself. For those of you who feel, "OK, I agree that it's reasonable to feel that way but for goodness sakes don't write about it! I write this as I feel there are others who could secretly identify with it. I must also admit that I have less control over my writing content than I would like! Anyway, for those people, who still are not convinced males should talk about feelings like this, I can only say that my parrot told me I had to write this!

Introduction

I grew up in the small town of Syosset, Long Island, New York. I perceived my peers through a 14-1/4" X 7" X 5" box that was my Courier 1M, Citizens Band radio. In 1962, something extraordinary happened in Syosset. Lafayette Radio Electronics Corp. (LRE) opened their flagship warehouse store on 111 Jericho Turnpike and Lafayette Drive. Lafayette Radio Electronics Corporation was the major store in the area that sold these magical machines called Citizen Band Radios. Although my particular radio was not of the LRE brand name, they did sell it and it appeared in their yearly 1962 catalog.

Lafayette Radio Electronics Corp. was my temple and its catalogs my bible. I read and reread each catalog issue hungrily, almost religiously every day. Each time I would study the catalog; I would glean another fact or find another radio accessory I had missed in my past searches. It gave me something to look forward to and equipment I could dream about. The radios and gear were our babies. They provided so much for us that we treated them with loving care. They provided the pathways to our friends and, what we considered to be, our family. It provided me the path from isolation and freed my soul.

Some of the stories denoted herein are based on real events. The names were changed to protect the innocent as well as the guilty. The places have been altered and situations elaborated, as is the writer's prerogative. The flavor of the thoughts and the feelings are real.

I write this book because of the profound influences Citizen Band Radio (CB radio) and the Lafayette Radio Electronics Corporation™ had on my life. It sounds strange when I read those last words over again even to me, but it is true. Perhaps it seems strange because it's not the CB radio that I've seen fictionalized on TV with the "Rubber Duck" and cast of other trucker characters. This story took place before the truckers adopted channel-19 and even before channel-9 was reserved for "React" and other emergency services. This is a story about coming-of-age in a small town and not being one of the "in-crowd." It is about young males being perpetually on the outside looking in without the communication skills to make friends and fit in. I guess it could be applicable to young females also but we knew little about those mysterious "alien beings" then.

I believe women are more genetically predisposed to be the communicators and men find it a lot harder to express and deal with their emotions, except for anger and violence. Our society encourages the stereotype of the stoic, protective male and the "little woman" who wears her emotions on the sleeve of her "Coco Channel®" blouse.

My genetic predisposition, being male, society's unspoken rules and the environment that I grew up in conspired against me. Males search for technological solutions to their problems where women talk them out with their friends. There is a saying something like "The difference between men and boys is the price of their toys." This rings true to me. Did you ever wonder why it fits? I have a "half-baked" theory that goes something like this.

Back in the good old cave dweller days, the men went out hunting and the women stayed home to take care of the little Neanderthals. The women could not meet their own needs as well as their babies (especially if she was pregnant) without communicating well with the other women of the tribe.

The bad communicators and their offspring died out as their essential needs were not met. The good communicators and their offspring prospered. I also think the women were pregnant a lot because of the lack of Cable, satellite TV, arm-chair sports, MTV, computers, and the Internet!

When the males came home from a hard week or so of bringing home the Mastodon bacon, they saddled up to their rock recliner around the fire with a cold one (melted ice) and had little else to do! It only took a couple of minutes (to do the real wild-thing!) There was no Masters and Johnson, adult video rental, petting, "Joy of Sex," Kama Sutra or Internet to check for tips. A couple of body slams, some fierce grunts, some groans and a huge sigh and it was nappy time, at least for the males. They even managed to get it in the right orifice part of the time. The other cave males that missed didn't have offspring to carry on their highly inaccurate aim.

I certainly hope we (as males) have become more educated and sophisticated in the art of lovemaking than this! We have, right, girls? You did hear me, didn't you? We have come a long way, right?

When the males went out on the hunt, they had to bring down the beasts like the Woolly mammoth. Some of the animals were much bigger and stronger and other animals were much faster and had keener senses of eyesight and olfactory prowess. There were no hospitals, doctors, or wonder drugs back then. You could die very easily from an infected scratch or bite. They needed some sort of Darwinian edge to survive. Each time they developed a new method of hunting, which gave them better odds at bringing home a huge "happy meal" with less danger to themselves, they insured their own survival as well as their little furry ones. Their need to communicate among themselves was only necessary to coordinate the hunt. Sign language, direction pointing, and a lot of grunting would suffice. In fact, this seems disturbingly similar to the modern male!

Rocks, sharpened spears, crude traps were the "high tech" toys of the day. The males spent may hours of their free time (when they weren't doing the wild thing) developing, honing and practicing with them. They were the tools of their trade. The other hunters, who did not seek to improve their odds were less successful and died out. I think this is the basis for males seeking a technological solution (their toys) to their problems and to supplement their fledgling communication skills.

CB radio as well as the Lafayette Radio Electronics Corporation was our "high tech" solution. It enabled our communication and helped create a path toward meeting and dragging our women back into our dens to make our own deposit to the genetic pool. I just hope none of those guys peed in it!

Seriously, CB radio saved my life as well as my mind. I feel they must have been as important to the lives of others.

Yes, it was a longtime ago, about 42 years ago from the start for me. I think it is about time for the story to be told. I think everyone has at least one story to tell and too many become lost when there is no one left to tell them. It is only when one within the group is a storyteller or at least seeks one out, will the story be documented for others to read.

I feel we are a product of our environment, which includes the people, places, and things where we grew up. I grew up with CB radio and the Lafayette Radio Electronics Corporation. They were vital in my matriculation to young adulthood.

I viewed the world through a speaker grill. This is a story of coming-of-age in a simpler, more innocent time. It was a time between wars. Vietnam hadn't heated up yet for us and terrorism was something that happened far away. It wasn't something we had to worry about in the safety of our country. Aids were something (or someone) you needed. There were audiovisual aids, hall monitor aids and teacher's aids. They were there to help, not to torture and kill you!

It was a good time in that a friend and a peer were always available at the push of a microphone button and the utterance of a few words. I think we were lost and trying to find our way. Instead, we found one another and finally a place where we belonged and felt accepted for who we were. In our desperate search for friends, companionship and love, we found something we weren't even looking for, ourselves.

I think, as we become adults, the barriers become more fortified and entrenched. You become more wary and friendship doesn't come as easy as it once did in your childhood and teenage years. I do know some wonderful exceptions but I believe they only confirm the rule.

I believe that our personality has developed in a series of shells like those Russian or Polish dolls, one inside another. The teenager is still there inside all of us. It may be a lot harder to reach for some of us than others, especially if you are working hard at playing the role of parent, husband, lover, manager, professional or some other mature role.

I also believe that if we are exposed to the proper stimulus, we can still contact our inner child or teen. I want to provide what I hope to be the correct stimulus and bring you back for a short visit to those formative years.

Some of you might be thinking, "Why would I ever want to do that?" You might feel this way especially if they were the painful, awkward years of growing into and feeling comfortable in your own skin. It was this way for most of us, although I think it was more painful for some of us than others.

I can think of several possible reasons for wanting to contact your inner teen. It is where our fun-loving playfulness comes from. It is a more honest and less complicated part of our personality. It is a place of unbounded creativity. It is a place of brainstorming without the analytical portion of your brain throwing figurative cold water on your dreams, aspirations, and fantasies. It was a time and place when anything was possible. It's a nice place to visit and linger awhile. It's also a way to get back into the mind-set of your own teenager. Sorry, I had to bring that one up!

It was a time when our ideals were less tarnished by experience. We were invincible and undefeatable and we were going to change the world! It was a place where our personality was forged. It was also a time of firsts. First day at a new school, first crushes, first loves, first car and first base. There were many seconds and thirds too! There is something special and magical about firsts. You can never have a second try at a first time. I know it sounds stupid but nonetheless true. I think you will have to supply the right answer for yourself.

Today's world is so complex and we are always rushing to our next appointment with the many places to be and people to see, sometimes we lose ourselves in the fray. I am a Tom Hanks Fan. One of my favorite movies is "Big." We don't have to be "Big" all the time, do we?

It is my hope, for those of you who grew up under the wing of the Lafayette Radio Electronics Corporation or the great CB radio era, that this book would be the right stimulus for you!

I started this book in 1995 and have worked on it sporadically since then. Recent events (9/11/01) have made me realize several things.

1) You may not have as much time as you thought you had. You can exercise, diet and plan to live forever and your life can be punctuated by the sound of shrieking, tortured metal, and falling concrete.

2) If there is something personally important to you, you owe it to yourself to do it now.

3) In these times it is sometimes necessary to escape from the 24/7 bombardment of news and videos of unbelievable tragedy and death. I do believe news is important and we have to make decisions, but we still need to celebrate the gift of life and laugh and have joy in our lives. If not, what would be the point of living? What would the prize be for succeeding?

I write this book as part of my catharsis, my escape from sadness and sorrow. I am a futurist. I thought naively the human race finally matured past the threat of nuclear war, the cold war and we were heading for a new age of enlightenment and innovation. I am disappointed with humanity. Ronald Reagan said something like this at least three times during his presidency, "How quickly our differences worldwide would vanish if we were facing an alien threat from outside this world." I no longer have that much confidence in the governments of the world. I think there would be collaborators if they could gain a personal or political gain for themselves, their family, their religious beliefs, or country no matter how short-lived. It could be the downfall of the human race

Sadly, I see a tough road of war and terrorist activity looming ahead. I see the threat of nuclear or biological war as being stronger than ever. During this writing, I can temporally forget about the world, which has been brutally thrust on us, and go back for a visit to the times of my youth. I hope I can make you see the world as I did back then and regain some of the joy and laughter I feel is so badly needed. It is my wish that this book will let you escape for a short time and enable you to rejoin the struggle replenished, renewed, and ready to handle the next great challenge our world may present to us.

So lie back on your favorite recliner and put your feet up. In your minds eye, put a nickel in the red, gas station vending machine. Open the door and pull out the dark, green-tinted, glass bottle of Coke® and pop the top on the opener built into the machine. Savor the ice-cold refreshing bite or, if you prefer, grab a pink can of Tab® and relax. Put a couple of Sen-Sens® in your mouth (did anyone ever like the taste of these?) Close your eyes, massage your temples briefly, take a deep breath, and let it out slowly. Do it once more and let it out slower. Shed the tension, high-pressure, and years like your pet shaking off water after a long needed bath and be ready to bask in the "Sunshine of your Love." Be ready to be transported back to the days long gone. Be ready to visit the days when Lafayette Radio Electronics Corp. and CB Radio were kings!

PS: Be sure to reopen your eyes to read this or else you will just fall asleep!

1 - The History of Citizen's Band Radio

In the Beginning There was...

The 11-meter band (26.960 – 27.230 megahertz MHz) was an amateur radio band, which was under utilized by the amateur radio community. In 1957, the FCC proposed reassigning this band to Class D use. Class D use was for noncommercial use by citizens.

In 1958, the 11-meter band was reassigned for Class D use and divided into channels 10 kilohertz (KHz) in bandwidth. The 23-channel CB band was born! The extra channel space between channels 22 & 23 resulted in the frequencies 22a & 22b being used as "pirate" frequencies. They became available for usage on some crystal-synthesized radios for "authorized" use only.

In 1957, an article was published in the Radio & TV news on how to construct a transceiver to use this new "Citizens Band." The industry capitalized on this early design and started producing the first kits with crystal-controlled transceivers. It was not until 1977 that channels 24 through 40 were added. The old channels 22a and 22b were used as channels 24 and 25 respectively and the rest of the channels were added. At one time, the FCC considered providing up to 99 channels. It was later decided that this might cause severe interference with the IF stages on many radio receivers and they scrapped this idea.

The CB radio channels and frequencies are denoted in the tables below. Some 23-channel CB transceivers had 22A & 22B capability but these frequencies were reserved. Although there was room for channels 3A, 7A, 11A, 15A & 19A, no CB radio could access them unless it had additional crystals added, a modification or a VFO (Voltage controlled Oscillator.)

Table of CB Channel and frequencies before 1977

CH-01	26.965	CH-011	27.085	CH-021	27.215
CH-02	26.975	CH-012	27.105	CH-022	27.225
CH-03	26.985	CH-013	27.115	CH-023	27.255
CH-04	26.005	CH-014	27.125	CH-22A	27.235
CH-05	27.015	CH-015	27.135	CH-22B	27.245
CH-06	27.025	CH-016	27.155	CH-03A	26.995
CH-07	27.035	CH-017	27.165	CH-07A	27.045
CH-08	27.055	CII-018	27.175	CH-11A	27.095
CH-09	27.065	CH-019	27.185	CH-15A	27.145
CH-10	27.075	CII-020	27.205	CH-19A	27.195

Table of Channels & Frequencies added to make 40 Channels

CH-24	27.235	CH-34	27.345
CH-25	27.245	CH-35	27.355
CH-26	27.265	CH-36	27.365
CH-27	27.275	CH-37	27.375
CH-28	27.285	CH-38	27.385
CH-29	27.295	CH-39	27.395
CH-30	27.305	CH-40	27.405
CH-31	27.315		
CH-32	27.325		
CH-33	27.335		

The road to hell is paved...

The Citizen Band Radio service was intended to be a place where everyday citizens could communicate. This could be during local events, emergencies, road trips, camping, accidents, and any other events, which the non-technical minded citizen might want to communicate on a noncommercial, local basis.

The Federal Communication Commission (FCC) regulated it. You would get an application for a license when you bought a CB set. You would fill it out, send in a nominal amount, and receive your license and call letters in the mail roughly 8 weeks later.

Amateur (also known as Ham radio) radio was a well-regulated international service that existed for many years before this. I think the FCC foresaw a local model of Amateur Radio for the less technical-minded citizen. They scaled down the power, frequencies, and requirements for a license and sat back to see what their handy work wrought. I don't think they had any idea what would come once they opened Pandora's famous box!

The Reality of CB Radio

The reality of CB radio was radically different from its intended use. Adults first tentatively used it as the equipment was hard to come by, expensive and you needed some technical expertise. Once the equipment became more cost-effective, easy to obtain and simpler to install and use, kids began to become interested. Kids began using their parent's CB radios at first tentatively like they were intended to be used. Kids are experts at pushing the envelope to see what their boundaries are. The kids cautiously began exploring the limits to see what would happen.

When the overextended FCC didn't punish them, they began to feel more confident. As more kids took over their parent's equipment, they began to dispense with the regulations and talk like they did in person to peers. It was like a local town-wide party line, which you could access from your car (or bicycle mobile!) It was the equivalent of the Internet, e-mail and the teen chat sites of today back in the 60's and 70's, but all local except for "skip."

It appealed to boys and they flocked to it by the dozens as it caught on. There was also a "pecking" order that put the kids with the best equipment, most experience, and best vocal skills (mostly put down skills,) at the top and the neophytes at the bottom.

You never know who is listening on a radio frequency but when you talked only to your friends, it was easy to forget this. The language they used was by far not the same as they used in front of teachers or parents.

Another one of the peculiarities of talking to local friends was you created a mental picture of people in your mind from their voices and actions. This was true even though many people didn't realize it. This image was so firmly entrenched in your mind when you met them, it was often more real than the image of seeing them in person. It took constant exposure to them in person, over a long period to dispel the image created by your mind from their voice over the radio. Sometimes it never happened and you kept your radio image of them when you talked to them on the radio. It doesn't make sense but, but sometimes the human mind has all sorts surprises in-store for us.

2 - THE RADIO EQUIPMENT

ANTENNAS

Most of as started out with 1/10 of a watt (100mw) walkie-talkies then graduated to 5-watt CB transceivers. It was a similar situation with antennas. I started out with a pair of LRE's HE-29Bs walkie-talkies my brother and I received for Christmas one year. Once I received a real 5-watt base station, I used an elbowed, loaded whip antenna on the back of my radio. I next went to a quarter-wave ground plane, which I inserted into the hole that was the former residence of the "merry-go-round" style backyard clothesline. My last antenna was a HyGain collinear mounted on the roof with a tripod. Other people went to rotating "beams" to provide directional gain and attenuate the people they didn't want to hear. There was an antenna called the "Super Scanner" which was supposed to give you the best of both worlds. It had three vertical elements arranged in a triangular pattern. This antenna could be electrically rotated. What I mean is it did not physically rotate but you could electrically co-phase any two of the vertical elements to give you some directional gain similar to a two-element beam antenna.

Transceiver and accessory Manufacturers

Here are some manufacturers and model names of Citizen Band radio, other equipment and accessories manufacturers sold for this CB use. The names are sure to bring back some memories

Action Laboratories, Aircastle, Airline, Alinco, Alliance, Allied, Alpha, Allstate, Ameco, Ameritron, Amphenol, Apelco, Applied Electronics, Arkay, Arvin, Astatic, Astron, Autek, Automatic, Biggs Electronics, B&K, B&W, Babcock, Bendix, Breting, Browning Labs, Burstein-Applebee, Cadre Industries, Capitol, Channel Master, Citizen Electronics, CDE, Central Electronics, Chickasha Electronics, Citizen Electronics, Citi-Fone, Clarostat, Claricon, Cobra, Collins, Commander, Concord, Courier (E.C.I.) , Conar, Dak, Davis Manufacturing Company, Daystrom Products Corporation, Demco, Dentron, Dewald, Dixon Electronics, Dowkey, Dragon, Drake, Dunlap Electronics, Duo Comm, Dynascan (Cobra), E.C.I.,Eico, Fannon, Echo, EDCO, Eddystone, Eico Electronic

Instrument Company, Fieldmaster, Eimac, Eldico, Elmac, Electro Voice, Electronic 2000, Electrophonic (Ross), GC Electronics, Geloso, Gem Marine, Gemtronics, General Electric, General Radio, General Motors, General Radio Telephone, Globe Electronics, Gonset, Gross, Hallicrafters, Hallmark, Hammerlund, Harvey Wells, Heathkit, Henry, Hickok, Hewlett Packard, Hy-Gain, Icom, ITT, James, J.C. Penny, Jonson, Kaar, Kenwood, Knight Kit, Kris, Lafayette (LRE), La Salle, Lincoln, Lloyd's, Lysco, Magnavox, Mark Products, Masco (Fannon), Maxon, Metrotek, Midland, Monitoradio, Motorola, Morse(Electrophonic), Olsen, Osborne, Pace, Palomar, Panasonic, Pearce-Simpson, Pencrest (J.C. Pennies), Philmore, Poly-Comm, Racal, Radio-Shack (Realistic), Ratheon, RCA, Realistic, Realtone, Regency, Robyn, Ross, Royce, Sampson, SBE, Sears, Sharp, Siltonix, Silvertone (Sears), Sonar, Sony, Spokesman, Standard, Squires-Sanders, SSBCO (Mark Products), Swan, Teaberry, Telcraft, Telecon, Tmc, Trio, Tram, Triplett, Triumph, Tructone, U.S.L, Utica, VEB, Vocaline, Wards, Waters, Webcor, Webster, Weston, World Radio Labs and Yaesu.

The Controls of a CB radio

Tunable receive – A smooth continuously adjustable receive control, which allowed you to receive all CB frequencies without crystals.

Channel selector (transmit) – A rotary selector knob which allowed you to select different transmit crystals (or just frequencies for the later frequency synthesized radios.)

Channel selector (receive) – A rotary selector knob that allowed you to select different receive crystals (or just frequencies for the later frequency synthesized radios.)

Channel selector (receive and transmit) – A rotary selector knob which allowed you to select different transmit and receive crystals (or just frequencies for the later frequency synthesized radios.)

Volume control - Usually a rotary control that allowed you to adjust the loudness of the received audio.

Squelch - Usually a rotary control that allowed you to adjust the relative signal strength necessary to allow a signal to pass to the speaker. It was used to quiet down the noisy channels for voices, carrier squeals (heterodynes) and electrical noise. This worked especially well when you wanted to talk to local strong signals only.

RF sensitivity - Usually a rotary control that allowed you to adjust the relative signal strength of received signals but did to squelch the audio.

Meters –

S-meter 1- S9 10, 20, 30, 40, 50 displays the relative strength of the received signal

RF power- indicated the output wattage of your radio. 5 watts input power was and still is the legal limit. Our tube radios could generally put out 3-4 watts.

Modulation - 0-100% and red zone – This is how much transmitting audio you were putting out. Anything over 100% was called over-modulation and caused interference on other frequencies, especially adjacent channel frequencies.

Speaker - This is where your receive audio emanated.

Microphone – This is what you spoke into which usually had a switch to change from receive to transmit modes. The D-104 (with and without built-in preamp), Turner amplified microphones and the Lafayette Electronics Corp. Radio Crystal bullet microphone (also known as the Green Hornet) were all popular models from this era.

Preamps (Preamplifiers) – These small amplifiers or compressors took the audio from your microphone and amplified it (boosted-it) before it was input into the microphone amplification stage of your radio. Later, some radios and microphones came with their own built-in preamps. Initially external preamps such as the Knight compressor-preamp C-577 by Allied Radio and the Vibratrol transistorized preamps were popular aftermarket add-ons of choice.

Earphone jack/Earphones – These gave you the ability to listen to the CB radio covertly or without disturbing your parents (both mentally and physically!)

External antenna – This is an antenna, which is outside the house, generally on the roof.

Coax – The concentric cable used to connect the radio to the antenna. It was usually RJ-8 or RJ-58U coax.

Linear Amplifier – A RF amplifier that takes the maximum of 5 watts input and amplifies it to 100 up to 1000 or more watts. They are and were strictly illegal for use on CB.

After Burners ON!

Sometime called a Linear Amplifier, afterburner, Kicker, Black-box and a multitude of another euphemisms which are names for illegal linear amplifiers. These devices, although legal for amateur radio, were and still are illegal for CB radio. They amplify the output power well beyond the allowed 5-watt input limit. Some amplify the output power to as much as 1000 & 2000 watts.

Some were thinly disguised as Amateur Radio amplifiers but were really intended for CB radio. Here are some of the linear amplifiers makes and models that might bring back some memories. The manufacturers and models numbers are listed alphabetically by name as follows:

ABC 7107, Afterburner, Ameritron AL80B, Amp Supply LK800, Antlafier, Apollo 300X/400X, Blackcat JB 1-SS, Blackcat JB 12, Blackcat JB 75, Blackcat JB 75A Mobile, Blackcat JB 76, Blackcat JB 76 Mobile, Blackcat JB 150, Blackcat JB 200A Mobile, Blackcat JB 2000 6, Blackcat JB 2000 80-10, Browning 170 Mobile, Browning 180, Boomer 250, Courier BL-100, Courier ML-100 Mobile, Crusader 300, D & A Bandit, D & A Bandit II, D & A Hawk, D & A Hornet, D & A Scorpion, D & A RaiderD, & A Maverick 250, D & A Falcon 400, D & A Phantom 500, Demco Demon 50, Demco Demon 50 Mobile, Demco, Demon 250, Demco Demon 500+, Demco A500, Dentron Clipperton L, Dentron GLA 1000, Dentron GLA 1000B, Dentron MLA 2500, Drake L-4 B, Drake L-7, Elkhart Swinger, Elkhart 500S , 1010S , 500SB , 1010SB, FireBird 500 Amplifier FireBird 500 dial-a-watt, Galaxy 600 , 800 , 1000, Galaxy 1500, Golden Falcom 2000, Heathkit HA10, Heathkit HA14, Heathkit SB200, Heathkit SB220, Heathkit SB221, Heathkit SB230, Henry 2K-2, Henry 2K-4, Henry 2K-5, Hygain Afterburner 420,

Golden Eagle 150 Mobile Amplifier Kenrich, Eagle 500, Golden Eagle 750, Golden Eagle 1KW, Knightkit T-175, Kris 200 mobile, Kris 200, Kris Mach 3, Kris Mach 3+3, Lafayette (LRE) HA250 Maco Mini-Brute, Maco 200 ,Maco 300, Maco 300 Mobile, Maco 750, Mirage B-23, Mirage C-211,Mosquito 50, Mohawk Electronics 2A, Mohawk Electronics 5B, Mohawk Electronics 7A, Mohawk Electronics 8A, National NCL2000, Pace PX 100, Pal 200MDX Mobile, Pal 201BDX Base, Pal 321, Pal 350MDX Base, Pal 350MDX mobile, Palomar TX 50, Palomar TX 75, Palomar TX 100,Palomar TX 150, Palomar 90a, Palomar 100, Palomar 160, Palomar 200b, Palomar 200m, Palomar 300, Palomar 300a, Palomar 310m, Palomar Skipper 300, Palomar 350z, Palomar HD 400, Palomar Elite 500, Palomar 500m, Palomar model 50, Palomar p150, Palomar Pulsor, PE 225, PE 500, Pocket Rocket, Pride DX 300 80-10, RF Concepts RFC2-117, RF Concepts RFC3-222, Shooting Star 225, White Tornado 225, Siltronix 550, Stam-Comm M100, Stinger 100, SuperStar 550, Swan 1200X Cygnet, Texas star 350, Texas Star 250, Texas Star 667R, Thunder Bolt 101, Thunder Bolt 305 and Varmit 450XL.

3 - Beginnings of the Misfits of Channel 10

It is not easy to remember and describe in detail, with total clarity and detachment, the events that forged your personality. I do not believe I want to describe all of them. Besides, some of them would not be interesting!

I am attempting to describe events that I feel were vital in my metamorphosis into young adulthood and how they felt to me. It is not an easy task to perform because actions, which seemed innocent then, may look different now in the cold, clear light of today's far less innocent and much more "Politically Correct" world.

It is not my intent to portray anybody as a juvenile delinquent. Some of us were misguided, maybe looking to do something to get some recognition from the other members of the group or sometimes just to cut the boredom. In addition, people are seldom (if ever) just good or bad.

All the people I talk about here I believe to be good people. We were kids in a more unenlightened and innocent society than today. Most of the time we were just looking for something different to happen, so one day would not be the same as the next. There weren't as many choices as there are to be today. There was no cable or satellite TV, cell phones, electronic games, personal computers, or Internet. Some of us didn't even have telephone privileges for incoming as well as outgoing calls. There wasn't even a chance for our own extension telephone. There was one B & W TV in the house in the living room.

You were lucky if the family acquired a Color TV. In those days, only a few programs had the "Peacock" and were in "Living color." There was that special switch in the back of the TV that let you put even Black and White programs in color! Well, that was the way it was represented. This was one of those "brilliant" marketing ploys that sold many TVs, but left the customers very cold. This was how we acquired our color TV.

Joe Huckster, sales and marketer supreme was demonstrating one of these new "wonder devices" at the Floyd Bennet Field shopping center. "Have you been waiting for you favorite TV shows like Amos and Andy, I Love Lucy, Lassie or other fine shows to be transformed into glorious color? Have you been waiting for this before turning out your hard-earned cash on a color TV that will only show you a meager few programs a day in full color? Well folks, I am, here today to tell you your wait it over! The answer to your dreams has been made available to you today through the miracle of modern science! This magical Color TV appliance will bring to you the wonderful opportunity to show all (as in 100%) of your TV shows and broadcasts in color! This is our 100% guarantee! When adjusted correctly and in good repair, if any one of your shows fails to be shown in color, you will get a full refund and you get to keep the TV for absolutely FREE as our gift to you!"

"Think of the money you will save on movie tickets! This huge 23" screen is like having a movie theater in your very own home! What do you have to lose? Look what you have to gain! Hurry, Hurry, Hurry! I am sorry folks but quantities are limited! If you order right now (and I know I shouldn't be doing this folks!) You will get the superb Color Tracker "rabbit ears" antenna absolutely free! But there's more! Have you been looking for an AM/FM stereo system with speakers? Those alone will run you hundreds of dollars! Buy the console version and get an AM/FM stereo and a high-end Record changer absolutely free! Buy it in the next 15 minutes and get FREE installation and delivery!"

Well that is how we acquired our first console stereo/color TV. We even received free installation and delivery! They installed it and turned it on and we had a "huge" 23-inch B & W picture. We asked the deliverymen about the special switch, our dad scowled at us, and we quickly moved out of "cuffing" range. My dad looked at the deliverymen expectantly. "Sir, here is the operator's manual. Be sure to read all the instructions before turning anything else on. The switch you want is in the back near the bottom of the TV." My father thanked them, gave them a tip and they left a vapor trail behind them, they left so fast. My dad took out his glasses and he began following with his finger as he read the manual and mumbled aloud. I started to ask about the color switch, "Why the heck didn't they just leave the TV in that mode? Why was there a switch to turn it off and on in the first place? Why wouldn't everyone want all of the programs in color? Then why would they put it way in the back near the bottom of the TV so it was hard to reach?"

"Stop bothering me and let me read the instructions!" My dad thundered with a blotchy red face. We all ran for the hills and our bedrooms. You didn't mess with my dad when he got like that! We peeked in later when he called us. Dad got the family gathered around and he moved the Console away from the wall. He had to stretch out on the floor behind the behemoth to reach for the switch. Then my father "demonstrated" it to us. "Here we go! Hold onto your hats! Watch this! You can now watch all of your TV shows in Full color!" My dad moved a little slide switch from the B&W marking to the "Sep." position marking.

"Well, how is it?" We looked at each other and made scared, bewildered faces. "Well how is it? He bellowed.

"Well, it didn't work!" I stammered out.

"What the heck!" he said and flicked the switch back and forth several times. We noticed the picture changing from B&W to a reddish tint.

"How is it now?"

This time nobody ventured a comment.

"God damn it, do I have to do everything around here myself!"

We decided it was time to leave again and we vacated the local premises.

Later, we found out the "Sep." stood for "Sepia." That meant a picture with less contrast and an awful pinkish-red tint. What about that "special" feature of turning 100% of our B & W programs into "glorious" color? Technically, it worked as promised although there was nothing "glorious" about it! The B&W shows we watched went from B&W to a drab tint of Sepia all through the "magic of science!" It looked terrible! Black and White mode had more contrast and was sharper. The Sepia switch also put a reddish tint on the few color programs and made them look bad also. My dad steadfastly refused to turn the switch back as we paid for the extra feature and we had darn well better get our money worth! I think he hated it as much as we did but if he conceded this point, it would be admitting that he had been duped. After the TV set had some mileage on it, the Sepia tint mysteriously disappeared one day. We asked once more about the "color switch" and became the target of his frustration and rage and we had "Sepia" TV for one more week. I made a pact with my family never to bring up the topic again or I know my dad would just turn it back on again!

We didn't have many of the technological wonders of today back then, no money and few choices. Since sometimes nothing seemed to be happening, we provided a little nudge. Sometimes those nudges were more socially irresponsible than others were. It was never the intent of any of us to cause physical harm or mental anguish to another human being. We didn't understand the cruelties of our actions. There weren't many social stars among our number. We were not involved in sports, school events, or clubs and didn't have many friends. Now you might be thinking, "Whose fault is that?" As fallible humans, we become trapped in prisons of our own making. It is also true that we hold the key. My prison was an airtight cell and my key was a speaker and a microphone. I perceived most of the following events through a speaker. It was either as it was happening or during a discussion of what happened afterwards. I don't recall a time that I was ever present in any of the events until much later.

Back in my early days, I was always interested in electronics. I was also a loner. I became involved with experiments with electricity and the family TV set at an early age. I always wanted a set of walkie-talkies. My brother and I received a set one year for Christmas 1962. They were Lafayette Radio Electronics Corp. Model HE-29Bs. They came with real leather cases, two crystal-controlled, channels and a huge telescoping whip antenna that when extended, cold also be used for "sword" fights! One of the two crystal channels provided was channel-10. My brother and I sometime heard other people talking on this channel but were never able to reach them.

Sometime later, I found out there was this hobby called "Amateur Radio" where experimenters built their own electronic equipment and then broadcast on them into the airwaves. They could contact other Amateurs with similar interests as well as foreign and exotic lands. I was ecstatic! I had to get a license and get into Amateur Radio! I started pestering my father to drive me into New York City (in those days, the test was only administered by the FCC in one location and you had to schedule it) to Varrik Street to take the test. I also kept telling him that I wanted a "Ham Radio." The year was 1963 and I was thirteen.

My father worked in a large aircraft company with many electrical engineers and a corresponding large number of "hams." One day the inevitable happened. My father came home with a surprise! He had something covered in newspaper, which looked heavy, peeking out of a supermarket grocery bag. I couldn't wait to see what it was! With some fanfare and flair he unveiled it. "Ta Da!" He said and pulled it out of the bag. It had a flat black front panel and a chromed outer case. It had military style, cast aluminum front-panel controls, rack handles and a black, hand-microphone. I looked at the front panel and it read, "Courier 1M Citizen's Band Radio." My father bought me a used CB set! So what do you do when you are offered a gift with the best of intentions? It wasn't an Amateur radio, but it was a two-way radio! I grinned and bore it! Sometime later on I found out the rack handles on the front panel, which assisted you in the removal of the radio from the case, were aftermarket add-ons. They looked like original equipment!

The CB rig was a vacuum-tube type in a military or aircraft style. It had a 23-channels plus tunable receiver and required a crystal for each transmit frequency. The transmitter had 12 crystals inside and an external socket for inserting an additional transmit crystal. It came with a little loaded telescoping whip with an elbowed PL259 that fit into the back of the transceiver.

I bought the transceiver up to my bedroom and plugged it in to the AC power outlet. I turned it on and watched it slowly light up with an eerie yellow-orange glow through the copious ventilation holes. I would know that glow intimately and learned to derive much comfort from it. I tuned through the dial and heard some people talking! Maybe this wasn't so bad after all!

I listened to the conversations and heard people using call signs. I heard calls like, "KKD2292, KKD6194 and KQD6140." I looked over the documentation supplied with the CB transceiver and found an application for a CB license. My dad filled it out (as you had to be 18) and sent it off. Through the next eternity of weeks, I listened and waited eagerly, checking the mailbox every day to see if the damn license would ever arrive!

I waited, listened, and learned the foreign language of this strange, new medium. I also learned the names, personalities and the call letters of all the local CB operators. Finally, a letter came from the Federal Communications Commission. I held it and stared at it. I could not open it. I was afraid of being disappointed if it was not my call letters. It was then I saw that it was addressed to my father! I couldn't even open it if I had wanted to! Due to the perverseness of the human mind, I now had the unbearable urge to tear it open and see if it was indeed my license! It had to be! It had been an unendurable eight weeks since I filled out the application and my dad mailed the paperwork!

The minutes passed like days, the hours like months. Would my dad ever come home? Finally, the moment arrived and I handed it to him. He looked at it, put it on the counter, and said, "I have to wash up for dinner." There it stood "screaming" out to me all during dinner. I stared at it for so long I could see it move. It beckoned to me like the Siren's song. Was I to be dashed on the rocks and disappointed? My future was less than seven feet away, separated from my eyes by a thin sheet of paper. I couldn't eat. My stomach was in knots. I keep staring at it as if I could glean what was inside just by concentrating hard enough on its countenance. I tried to zero and zoom in on the "Rosetta" stone that held the key to releasing me from my self-imposed banishment from the human race.

Suddenly, it was snatched from my view. "Let's see, what we have here," my father said as he sheared off an end of the envelope with a kitchen knife and put on his glasses. He blew open the envelope and removed the contents. He mumbled to himself as he read it and I held my breath. He then put his glasses in his shirt pocket with disgust. "Oh, just more junk mail!" My heart plummeted and leaped out my mouth at the same time. "It's just your CB license," he said as he dropped in on the counter and left!

I was the proud owner of KMD7264! I listened to the radio and waited for my opportunity. Every time I had one, I chickened out! Here I was, finally able to talk on this wonderful box and I couldn't do it! The words just seized up in my throat! I would just continue to listen and never be able to talk! Just when I was thinking this, there was another pause in the conversation. With electricity dancing through my nerves, I grabbed the black, hand-microphone, depressed the push-to-talk button with my thumb, and impulsively inserted my call letters. Nothing! They ignored me! I tried multiple times, each time with the same results! They acted like I wasn't there!

I tried sporadically after that without much enthusiasm and without any better results. This CB set was too old and all used up! One day I heard a strong signal in conversation with another group and I banally inserted my calls.

"Hold it a minute guys, go ahead KMD7264" I froze. I was heard! What the heck did I do now?

"Pick it up KMD7264!" came the slightly annoyed voice. I pushed the mike button and parroted what I had heard many times before and asked for a signal report. A guy named Dan gave me a report of S5 and the other two asked him whom he was talking to! They didn't hear me! I then found out about the usefulness of outdoor antennas and the Lafayette Radio Electronics Corporation (one of the only places in the area that sold Citizen Band Radio Sets, antennas and accessories.)

4 - The Misfits

How were each of the guys a misfit and what attracted them to CB radio? Don although stocky, was short for his age. Dan was of normal build but unsure of himself. Ted had a domineering mother that refused to let him grow up and I had a pair of proverbial "coke bottle glasses," an excessively protective, paranoid mother and no clue on how to interact with my peers. I had a social void in my brain. I was not allowed to interact with other kids, which I believe, exacerbated a genetic tendency toward bad social and communicative skills. I had logic and analytical skills which enabled me to try to untangle the unwritten and evolving (as you and your peer group matures) social cues and responses I needed to blend in and interact successfully.

The Survivor (Bob)

I think CB radio was attractive to the misfits. It is not that we looked like Quasimodo. Well, maybe some of us did! Nevertheless, we felt like it inside to a certain extent. At least I did. I am making many assumptions here. I strongly felt the duality of the conflict between inner feelings that contrasted with outer appearances. I felt broken, twisted, and removed from reality. I was looking at life through a hidden video camera. I could see and hear but I was never there. I was ignored. I remember several times getting the almost irresistible urge to jump up and down in front of someone and wave my hands. I began to wonder if I had the ability to become invisible. I began to look at my arms and legs as the controller of a remote diving robot might look at the robot's appendages and transducers that would sense data. I could look at my appendages, control them, and even pick up some data about temperature and other parameters but I never felt as if I were there. I doubted my own existence. Sometimes, I even doubted the real existence of this world. Granted some of it had to do with the awkward stage of turning into a teenager and dealing with hormones. Other parts had to deal with growing up in a dysfunctional family.

Hormones hit me hard. I had hair sprouting all over my body, even in some places hair was definitely not supposed to grow! I discovered my new toy early and proceeded to need a continuous re-tread on it throughout my school years. I needed to experience the "big O" six to ten times a day or I couldn't seem to function. A couple of times before school, in the bathroom at school, soon as I got home from school and a couple of times so I could sleep at night. Otherwise, my mental processes would become all jugged up with hormonal reactions and I felt that I would be a danger to society.

Girls at school would drive me nuts, but I would never approach them or even let anybody see how it affected me. The other guys were always late to class because they were smoking. Well I was late because I was "smoking too!" I was always hot! I was a muscular heavyweight but I wore very thick eyeglasses, which I hated. It was before contact lenses became affordable. Hard lenses were around, but in the $700.00 price range. They were far out of the reach of my meager finances.

My glasses looked like the proverbial coke bottle bottoms were cut and stuck in a frame. I am legally blind without some form of corrective lenses. For a while, I thought the old adage was true, but it never stopped me! At least I didn't go totally blind! The glasses added to my mental patient look. I was self-conscience about my glasses and was very introverted. I wasn't a bad looking guy but neither was I gorgeous. I did have a muscular body. However, I was an emotional cripple. My brain worked in ways that seemed intrinsically different from all the people around me. Part of it was due to a very paranoid mother. Sometimes I still ponder if I have some sort of different brain structure that causes me to think too much.

I was not allowed to stay after school, participate in sports, go out with the guys, have anyone over or make or accept telephone calls. I was always an outsider looking in. According to my mother, everybody was out to get us. I would never talk in school. I would listen but never express an opinion. The wheels were always turning, sometimes relentlessly so. I felt I was destined to be a loner. CB was my only contact with the real world. The image I projected on CB radio was flat and two-dimensional. That was typical. At least I projected something other than being a mental patient and, it enabled me to "see through a window" to the outside world.

As time progressed, a small circle of radio contact "friends" developed from nearby towns. I was known as "Bob in Syosset" because, at the time, I was the only Bob in the town that had a CB radio. Handles weren't used at first. It was all call letters at that time.

Handles came later on. We were preadolescent kids and most others that weren't, acted like them. There were plenty of characters.

There was Barry who came across as sounding lecherous and always wanted a Corvette. I think he saw it as the glamorous accessory that would make him popular with women and his fellowman. Then there was Dan AKA AstroCookie, Mark AKA Starship, Don AKA Air-Raider, Ted AKA the Night Owl and our beloved Henry who always talked about the Rangers hockey team. There was also Harry who was a 35-year-old mentally challenged man that fit right in, and a host of others.

We grew up with our small community of friends. We used to keep the CB set on constantly (with the squelch up) and "monitor" our favorite channel, Channel-10, which "belonged to us." I think, in other circumstances we could have started a gang. Me? I had no handle until much later. I adopted the handle "The Survivor" for reasons no one else knew. This is the first time I ever even brought it up. I was in mental anguish most of the time. I constantly thought of suicide.

I never thought I would survive Jr. High, then High School. I wanted desperately to put myself out of my misery. Most human beings need a validation of their existence. Normally this comes from a natural birthing process through society. Mine was an abortion. I needed interaction with others on a more personal scale. I needed contact with another mind. I had no clue how to accomplish this in person. CB radio provided this vicarious contact. It is an interesting concept though. Once you stare down into the inky depths of nothingness, what can life do to you? It is a hard idea to grasp, not existing for the rest of infinity. It is humbling and makes life's daily problems seem insignificant. It also makes religion very enticing. Nonexistence for infinity is hard concept to embrace and the mind blanches and runs away shrieking from its black tendrils. I think it is an important realization in the life of an individual. I think this realization comes eventually. The only problem is that later it is too late to do anything about it. If it comes sooner, it can help put you in touch with yourself so you can better plan how to spend the remainder of your, meager, allotted, possible century of existence. It is also a hard concept to maintain. It is easy to lose sight of it and have the everyday pains and pleasures seduce you back into the basic survival state or the path of least resistance. How many things do we do because society has taught us we have to do them? How much programming has our mind accepted through friends, family, society, school, religion, radio and TV, etc., before we had the proper techniques to critically evaluate the data stream?

Our worst enemy can be our own mind! It has been programmed in areas we normally can't reach. If we try to touch those areas, we are warned off, and then threatened by our own mind! What has civilization done to us? To explore and critically evaluate these areas is a painful process but the possible rewards can be liberating. What really matters? There is always a readily available alternative if things got too tough. Death was my security blanket. I guess it was just an extremely flammable one! It enabled me to walk outside of myself and transcend my prison. It set me free and let me enjoy life. How important is any day-to-day problems when placed against the yardstick of an eternity of nothingness? Death will happen soon enough, and I feel it is forever. There you don't have a choice There are no second chances. Your life is what you make of it, good, bad or just indifferent. I became "The Survivor," because I was constantly surprised I survived as long as I did! I never anticipated living through high school.

The Air-Raider

The CB microphone, like the motor vehicle, made powerful monsters out of some shy kids. They created an alter ego that was sometimes everything they wanted to be. They became tough and "eight feet" tall. The more power, the louder the audio, the bigger they appeared. Don (The Air-Raider) was the worst offender. He was always trying to make the ultimate microphone preamplifier that would make him sound "huger than life" He sounded loud and he acted big over the radio. He would back other kids into a corner and make them back down before there was ever a physical meeting or confrontation. His audio had power and even though it was over-modulated and splashed across the spectrum of CB frequencies, it never sounded distorted. I think his old LRE tube CB set allowed him the extra deviation without making him sound unrecognizable. It did make him sound huge!

He built the first preamp from a commercial 3-transistor circuit design. Then he would keep removing and substituting components to minimize the number of parts and maximize the audio. Don was always testing his audio creations on the air. I remember most of his airtime sounded like this. "How do I sound from now 1 2 3 to" CLUNK! (The loud sound of his toggle switch making the mike stand resonate.) "TO NOW 1 2 3!" His original audio was good and his amplified audio was thunderous!

The Starship

I have known Mark the longest and I trust him the most. Mark has never lost contact with his inner child. I say this and mean this in the best possible way. He is honest, straight forward and one of the most guileless people I know. Mark always had a strong persona on the radio but he never tried to be that much bigger than life. He was always friendly and up for fun. He would sleep with the radio on with the squelch up. I think you could have called him at 3 AM on a weekend and convinced him to go for a ride or a burger as long as it was for a friend that needed company or just to talk. He also loved those small White Castle® burgers and could easily be convinced!

He always liked (and still does) to laugh and make others laugh. He is also a practical joker and loved all those little tricks you could pick up at "the Magic shop." One of his favorites was (and still is) the stink bomb. The best ones were a little glass vial of concentrated stink! These vials are made from glass rods that are melted sealed on each end. They are about ¾" long and less than ¼" in diameter and pack an unbelievable punch! You could clear out a store in a hurry with one of these babies!

You have to smell one of these things to believe how strong they are! He would place them in either precarious places or under something (toilet seat, gum wrapper etc.,) so they would be crushed eventually. He would then stand far enough away, as to not be involved, but close enough to catch the action. The higher the society function the better. I guess this was his way of thumbing his nose at society.

The stink these little gems create is legendary and unbelievable! This is a case where smelling is believing! If you ever witnessed the excavation of a cesspool on a hot summer's day, then you would have some idea how bad these can really reek! You just can't believe how they could get so much concentrated stench in such a small capsule!

The Night Owl

The Night Owl acquired his handle from his proclivity of always being available on the air into the wee hours of the morning on weekends. Ted was a thin kid with dark-rimmed, plastic-framed glasses. He had a domineering mother that always belittled him (unintentionally, I think) in front of the guys.

He started what we called the "Night Owl club."

The Night Owl club was just a bunch of guys who would stay up late at night on a weekend. We would watch old SCI-FI and horror movies mostly of the cheesy type and make what they thought were funny comments on the radio.

H-Base

Harry was a mentally challenged man in his mid to late 30s. He was a good guy. We goofed around with him and sometimes made fun of him, I hope in a mostly nice way. We accepted him in our group. He didn't physically hang with us but he spent much time on the airwaves. He sounded like a younger guy and had a distinct, affected voice. He also took a little longer (sometimes a lot longer) to get the joke when we were fooling around. We didn't realize how "old" he was until we met him one day! He had a Richard Nixon 5 o'clock shadow and almost looked as old as our parents!

AstroCookie

Dan was one of the nicest guys. He was always for giving the new guys and novice CBers help. He was polite, affable, and helpful. He was mostly the voice of reason and staying calm. It is not to say that you couldn't get under his skin. Barry was especially skilled at doing this without trying! He made it look so simple!

Hotbox Mobile

Some of the guys we knew on the radio had sisters. When they found out it was a good place to meet guys, they made up handles and came on by themselves. There was a young woman with the handle "Hotbox Mobile" that started driving around through our neighborhood. She was a real tease. She would have all the guys salivating over the air. Starship wanted to meet her in the worst way. C'mon, we all know what the worst way is! She had a beautiful voice over the CB. I was more leery. I had already met some of the girls with beautiful voices. None of them fit my preconceived expectations. They, like us, were the misfits and the outcasts in either looks, physical features or emotional mind-set.

Starship finally met Hotbox Mobile. To my surprise, she was a very beautiful, well-endowed, voluptuous young woman, but she was also emotionally crippled. She wanted to be liked and more, to be loved. Starship wanted sex (we all did! I mean come on we were teens with raging libidos!) He had an even greater need to be attached. He wanted a girlfriend. I couldn't even imagine that stage for myself yet. If I could hold a girl still enough to "have my way with her" that would have been a good start!

Hotbox Mobile was not the attaching kind. She was a party girl and, I think she confused sex with love. It was his first time with an aggressive young woman that was a nymphomaniac. He was smitten. He couldn't understand what was going on. He was in love. She let him touch her bountiful breasts and become more intimate. She must be his girlfriend! Well it didn't work that way and she left her indelible mark on his psyche. It's one of the experiences that comes with the coming-of-age. That's why I become nostalgic thinking about it. I wasn't susceptible to that kind of "entrapment" only because I grew up with an overbearing mother who constantly yelled at my father and put him down. I made many promises a longtime ago that no woman was ever going to treat me like that. I was a nice guy until a woman raised her voice or in some other way hit one of my "hair-triggers." There was an instant drop in the temperature, as my blood became "liquid-nitrogen" cooled. I would never allow myself to get caught-up in a relationship with a woman I could love. I felt that it would mean dropping my barriers and giving up control. In my mind, I would be setting myself up for the very situation, I promised myself, in which I would never become involved. That is the way I felt. I am not saying it is the right way to feel. It is just the way it was. I missed many good opportunities with many wonderful young women because I would never let anyone in. If they tried to get in too hard, they would trip my defenses and I would get angry with them and drop them like last week's dirty laundry. Believe me, you would drop my last week's dirty laundry real fast!

It took a long while for me to let down some of my barriers and let somebody in. We all still have those hidden land mines and hair-triggers that come into play if someone treads in an area that is particularly sensitive because of past history. Most of us grow up and survive despite our childhood but there are remnants that never go away.

I grew up with CB. I crossed the indefinable, flexible barriers between prepubescent adolescent to young maturity on CB radio. When I discovered that I could be very successful with women, I left it all behind like a snake sheds it skin. I regret this now. I missed many good times and friendships. I spent all the extra time I had in search and pursuit, of pussy. I became obsessed with it. What if I wasn't at the local club and missed a good-looking woman? The time that I wasn't in search mode, I was working on refining my image. What did a woman want? What made a woman horny? I targeted myself to be more successful. I got better and better at it. I was obsessed. I became the nymphomaniac's counterpart. I was extremely lonely too. I wanted love but was afraid that I couldn't afford to pay the price. I was also a sucker for the lonely, different girl. If I saw somebody who wasn't dancing or seemed apart, they became irresistible for me. I wanted to make them feel happy. I guess it was a reflection of how I felt, and since I couldn't fix myself, I felt better when I fixed somebody else. I was drawn to the misfits, the pregnant, the emotionally troubled, and the lonely.

I got caught up in relationships where I became the parent, confessor, psychiatrist and counselor or it was just a sexual relationship. I never allowed my true self to show. Whenever someone dug too deep, I became angry and broke it off. I just wanted to make someone happy since I was broken inside in places I could not touch. It felt good to make someone else happy but I should have known it could never last and the breakup would be even more painful. I never expected to find someone with whom I could share my inner feelings, so I fortified the walls and set alarms and traps. I thought this kind of relationship would suffice. The truth is it is never enough. I had been alone before and I still was. It is one thing being alone and being lonely, it is indefinitely worse being with someone and feeling an even deeper loneliness.

Island Girl

Island Girl was another young lady who often passed through our area. She sounded real cute and she was a tease. She had all the guys foaming at the mouth. Mark was in the lead and finally did meet her. She was another beauty! Go figure! She was 5' 8", thin but curvy with long brunette hair. She was beautiful but shy in person as opposed on her "on-the-air" sexually aggressive persona. Mark tried desperately to have her stand up to her reputation but he couldn't get to "first base" with her. She was not that kind of girl! She only let the "inner slut" out to play when she felt that it was completely safe! She was playing at Halloween and she was wearing "the slut" costume but that's all it was. She was sweet, quiet, and very confusing to the guys.

The New Cadre

There was a group of "Adults" that thought they owned the local CB airwaves before the new cadre (us) made our appearance. They had been the owners by default. Now we were the intruders that tried to seize their throne and they didn't like it. We called them the "Old Farts" club. They seemed ancient to us! Mac was the ringleader. He was an old, stereotypical, beer-guzzling, construction worker that wanted to "beat the shit outta us." It was the duty of our group to provoke him.

It was a contest to see who could get closer to doom, count coup and live to recount the tale endlessly on the radio. Members of the group would drive past his house and lean on the horn at three o'clock in the morning. They did this while being on the airwaves. They would talk about it later, on channel-10. Looking back, it really wasn't smart to provoke this kind of friction intentionally. The weird thing is all of us are now older than he was then!

As inexperienced kids, I guess we figured this game of "cat and mouse" would last forever just as it was. As adults, we sadly known nothing is forever. Things and people change. People get older and finally die of old age if they were lucky enough to beat the odds and finally succumb to geriatric attrition.

Mac was older and more experienced. He upped the ante on the game to make sure it came to an abrupt halt. Mark decided it was his turn to play "the game" early one morning. "Hey guys listen to this!" Mark said over the "air" while in front of Mac's house. Mark gave three long honks then we heard, "Holy Shit," the revving of his engine and the screeching of the tires as he popped the clutch. Mac was there waiting for him. He had been hiding in his car, and as Mark passed by, and bleated on the horn, Mac's head popped up. The chase was on! Mark had always prided himself on his superb driving skills. He was driving a hopped up Chevrolet Vega. He had been the winner of many road rallies and he often practiced his emergency stops, power shifts, and 180-degree turns using his handbrake. This time his driving skills were put to the supreme test. Mark did not have enough time to put his driving skills to the test and talk on the radio at the same time. In addition, he didn't know if Mac was listening in for clues to where he was heading. This resulted in a dangerous high-speed chase through town that lasted for 45 minutes. Mark ended up getting far enough ahead of Mac to enable him to make a sharp turn unobserved. He screeched into a driveway and turned off the lights. He saw Mac pass by at high-speed.

"Pull over and lets settle this man-to-man! Ya little fucking coward," Mac commanded on his CB radio. It was Mac and he was obviously confused. It was then that inspiration hit Mark.

"You sound confused! But then what do expect from a guy whose parents are brother and sister?" Mark responded back.

"Why you fucking little ass wipe! Pull over so I can wipe up the street with ya!"

"Why don't ya make me? Have you followed the family tradition or didn't you have a sister to marry?"

"Son-of-a-bitch! Pull it over now!"

Mark couldn't resist any longer. He decided to back out and see whom Mac thought he was talking to and following. He was curious to see what was going on. He turned to follow the same direction Mac had gone when he had flown by.

He went a couple of miles and saw two cars pulled over off the on the side of the road, their lights were still on.

He slowed down to get a good look as he passed by.

It was unfortunate for the couple that had been peacefully driving down the road, minding their own business. Their only transgression was to be driving the same make, model, and color car as Mark's. They were severely shocked by the maniac that forced their car off the road! Mark rolled down the window as Mac was profusely apologizing to the older gentleman and his wife.

"Are you guys OK? I have a CB radio in the car and I can call the police on that maniac! I think he is an escaped child molester!" He couldn't talk any further as he erupted into laughter!

Mac whipped around, Mark waived, tooted on his horn, and burned rubber out of there!

Starship Invasions

When I was 17, I was lucky enough to secure a summer job working in the local mall as a security guard. I found it was a great way to meet women! My first "meeting" with Starship came during this time, although neither of us knew it at the time. I had a 5-watt 3-channel LRE walkie-talkie (which I still have,) that I used to keep in contact with other guards (when they had radios.) I also used it to listen-in to the "channel-10 boys." Well I got a call about a shoplifting in Sterns, which was at the other end of the mall. I started to run down the crowded mall. My radio was on and belted to my side. As always happens when you try to do too many things too fast, I tried to turn the volume down but since the HT was orientated facing away from me, I turned it the wrong way.

There used to be a satirical cartoon on in those days called "Super Chicken." There was a jingle played in the beginning of the show. It started out with the Calvary "charge" song usually played on a trumpet. They played it on a kazoo or toy trumpet and it sounded sickly. "Da ta, da ta, da ta, da ta, daaa. When there are signs of trouble, and you need help on the double, you just callll Super Chicken, Cluck Cluck, Cluck, Cluck! Just calll Super Chicken, Cluck Cluck Cluck, Cluck!" Well it seems that someone recorded this jingle and had the great timing to play it over and over "on the air" at this moment in time. The more I struggled to retain my handcuffs, nightstick, and composure and lower the volume, the louder it got. I ran through the center of the mall down towards the far end jingling and trying to hold onto my equipment blasting out the Super Chicken jingle the whole way. It was my most mortifying experience until that time and some time after!

When I talked to Dan later that week and told him about the incident, I told him if I ever found the @#$%^&* person who played it, there would be a death in his family. What I didn't know was Dan recounted the story to Mark and Mark made him swear he would never tell me he was the purveyor of this dastardly deed! I knew Mark then but not as well as I did later. I took myself too seriously back then. It was many years later that I found out Mark played this sound clip over the air.

Mark was always one for recording weird stuff, conversations, jingles, strange and obscene sounds and playing them over the air. It became one of his trademarks. Even today he has many tapes that were recorded live "on the air" from the old days. He has many audiocassettes of actual CB conversations from those days that he transcribed onto audio CDs. It is an eerie feeling listening to conversations that occurred 35 or more years ago, especially when you hear your own voice (which always sounds different then you hear it) saying things you don't remember saying! We sounded so young. I didn't remember us sounding so young. I guess your memory leaves out those kinds of details, the stuff that changed gradually so they always seemed to be the way they are.

Mark likes to make people laugh. He is the prankster. He'll do about anything for a good laugh. He is still very much the practical joker today. He was on an important date with his fiancé when he pulled a typical one. It was the first time his mother met his fiancé's parents. They went to a Chinese restaurant. He managed to slip away with a fortune cookie and he inserted a phony, gross fortune. He then slipped it back in place at his fiancé's side. He then convinced everyone to read their fortunes aloud without privately reading them first. The message had to do with the sexual act he hoped for when they got home. Rosemary read it aloud before she realized what it said. She became thoroughly embarrassed and Mark had his fun.

Mark had a boss once that he considered a "real prick" So, to this day, he sends him a birthday present on his birthday. It is a plain birthday card with a condom inside tied in a knot. The inside is filled with some semi clear dish washing fluid. He made it look like somebody had a good time!

Early on, Starship became a printer. He could print up just about anything. One day, he was not too busy at work and he became inspired by the Ken Kanumic family. He had taken a picture of Ken early in the morning after a long night of drinking. Ken's eyes were bloodshot and he had serious black circles and bags under them. They were rolling around in his head trying to roll back up so he could lapse back into blissful unconsciousness. His face was sporting what looked like several days growth. His hair, unruly to begin with, pointed out in random directions. In the photo, his eyes had a crazed, fanatic look. He looked like something between a terrorist, a cult leader and a bowery alcoholic. It was a striking (in a spooky way) yet unflattering photo. You would want to hide the children and lock up the "womenfolk" if you saw the likes of him wandering around your neighborhood! You might also want to load the shotgun!

Ken's nickname was "Turk." Mark took Ken's picture and printed up a 1000 posters with his picture on it. He posted them throughout the whole neighborhood. It proclaimed, "ELECT TURK KUNUTSIE CHIEF." In smaller letters underneath it said "Cause of pollution!"

The more the family tore them down, the more he posted. He then started getting creative. He would put 50 staples all over the face of the poster to make them more difficult to get down. Only a small piece would come off at a time. He then experimented with height. He stood on the roof of his car, and posted them at the full extent of his reach. He got them up close to almost the 11-foot level!

Ken's father tried balancing on the top of a ladder to pull one of the sky-scraping posters down. It was also one of the 50-staple varieties, which only let you rip off a small piece at a time. He was so angry when he finally got it all off; he forgot he was still on a ladder. He stepped off the ladder and was laid up in the hospital with a broken back. We visited him in the hospital but his heart monitor started making fast beeping sounds like a mad chipmunk on speed. It turned out that these were the sounds of an overstressed heart just before a cardiac arrest, so we had to leave. We thought he would be glad to see us!

5 - Daily life on the radio, our reality

I often try to recall and, I am don't remember what the heck we talked about on the radio for all those "man-hours!" I guess it was idle chitchat. I do remember talking about outstanding events that occurred in school and the tight sweaters that made them stand out! We talked about TV and the shows we liked best, kids that got suspended, or acted up in class. We also spent much time posturing and setting the rules of dominance. There was no physical body comparison that could be made on the radio. It all depended on how you sounded. The louder, deeper and the stronger voices usually dominated. The guys with better verbal fencing "put down" skills were up there too. Dan was a "put down" artist and Don had a deep, booming audio. Mark was a combination of both. It created a "pecking order." Newbie's always started out on the bottom rung unless they showed cause to be otherwise. I guess there were moments of scintillating conversation but mostly it wasn't anything too important, It was just good to have a peer to talk to.

Sometimes you made a connection and you made more than just a radio buddy, you made a true friend. These were more likely to occur in the midnight hours when the bullshit ran dry and true thoughts and feelings emerged. You would get so tired that you didn't have the energy or the speed of thought to come out with a witty or snide comment. It was almost like being plied with truth serum. I had a naturally deep voice and it got deeper as I relaxed or got tired. I wasn't one for posturing and looking to make my image larger than life. Maybe it was because I was already a big guy. I was more interested in getting past all the bullshit and contacting someone else's true thoughts and feelings. It was one of the reasons I became a founding member of the "Night Owl club." It wasn't really a club but we had a group on Friday and Saturday nights that would stay up late watching TV and keep one another company. There was magic in those midnight hours. It was during those times we bonded and made our closest friends. It was a sad thing to see it go as we gained wheels, dates, and places to be on these "premier" date nights.

I was one of the ones that left to go in "pursuit of." In retrospect, I am sad to see the male bonding, quality time end. We let our guard down more on CB radio in the midnight hours. Maybe it was because we would not normally be in each other's company when we were that tired and our guard was down. Maybe because we weren't in physical proximity so there was no male dominance issues. Whatever the reasons for it, it was something I enjoyed. It gave me a warm sense of belonging and a calmness of soul that I had never felt before. It was when the most special times occurred. The only things I can presently compare with that feeling is when I am writing, after a taking a hot shower after a heavy workout at the gym, or after having a satisfying sexual encounter. I have spent many hours on different Amateur radio bands trying to recapture those moments. I am sad to finally realize that you can't recapture your past. It was a different time and place. It is a nice, warm, place to visit and reminisce about. I don't think I would want to live there again. Maybe if I knew then what I know now... Well that will be covered in another book!

The Allure of the Microphone

What was the allure of CB radio anyway? It affected people differently. It made some kids with feelings of inadequacy into Gods (at least in their own minds.) It gave social outcasts a tenuous link to society. It was our hot line. We could always talk to someone there. You never felt alone. Maybe we didn't discuss our innermost feelings most of the time but we did meet other kids who had similar needs for companionship and kinship. We talked and sometimes even communicated. It wasn't always what we said. There was always a lot of nonverbal communication expressed in pauses, inflections, and emotional inflection. The content was of the least importance. How many people do you know who would spontaneously stay up all-night with you just to trade banalities and watch old movies? I think it filled an important sociological niche. It prevented us from turning to drugs, gangs, and crime. Well, at least it helped to prevent some of us from turning to crime! It provided us with identity and a family that was always available. It gave us the ability to meet new people and interact with them. This was especially important to me and I imagine other "shut-ins." It was our lifeline and our link to others who let us know that we were not alone. Not being exposed to other kids, feeling different and broken inside and never meeting another mind besides your own and those of your paranoid parents, makes you take everything too seriously. Some people might argue that CB caused people to become more isolated as we did not have to go outside to experience the world. We could have vicarious interaction by remote control. This was the case for me for a while, but it gradually changed. This may have happened to others, but if it did, it was my experience that it was the exception. I was locked away more than anybody I knew. Making friends and hearing about other kids lives, gave me something to compare to my own life. It also gave me the strength to transcend it. It may have taken me awhile but I did break the bonds of isolation. I am not an outgoing person by nature and I will never be one. It is still hard work for me to be in a social situation, but I can handle it. It doesn't come to me easily and it's not natural. I can analyze the situation and usually come up with a socially acceptable response. Sometimes, I can even enjoy it! The more social interaction I have, the easier it becomes for me and the more I can enjoy it.

My wife is a natural at social interaction. She can make the most inapt social misfit feel at home. She keeps the conversation going and always knows the right thing to say. I guess that is how we meshed. She made me feel comfortable and I listened. I am a good listener.

I think the CB radio phenomenon, as I knew it, is over. I think it has been replaced with newer modes of indirect-contact, communication such as computer chat rooms and "Surfing the Internet." This has both positive and negative connotations. In one way, you're at least two more steps removed from direct interaction.

1) You type messages back in forth not in real time. Of course, there are "Instant Messenger" type services available now. There is no voice interaction and you have no clue about the age or sex of the person with whom you are communicating.

2) You can be, and most probably are, in a different part of the country than the person you are communicating with so the chances of a direct physical meeting are much smaller.

In another way, since there is less chance of a physical interaction, you feel free to express what you feel. Writing lets you revise what you write until you feel it is an accurate representation before committing it to the four winds. This can and has lead to more permanent types of relationships. Like every new type of technology, there are those who look toward it as a weapon of choice to take advantage of the young, old, the less experienced and more innocent.

The Care and Feeding of our newborns

I spent much my time listening and talking on the CB radio. My Courier 1M was my baby. It was my portal to my real existence. I kept it in tip-top shape. I kept the outside chrome and metal knobs shinning bright with Noxon liquid metal polish and lots of old-fashioned "elbow grease." Noxon came in a green can with an off-white pop-top. The liquid itself looked like melted Vanilla-Bean ice cream but it had a strong caustic odor. I am sure it didn't taste like ice-cream either although I never put it to the test!

I took care of the inside components of the radio also. If there was possibility a tube was getting gassy or weak, I would take them down to LRE or Electronic City and test them on their tube testers. Lafayette Radio Electronic Corporation was located on 111 Jericho Turnpike in Syosset. It was a main warehouse store. It was too far to walk and close to the limit for a bike ride. Electronic City was located in the only mall within biking distance, in Mid-Island Plaza in Hicksville. When I tested a tube, if the meter needle wasn't full into the green, I would consider replacing it. I say consider, as I did not have unlimited funds at my disposal and I sometimes put off replacement until my next allowance. If it was an emergency and I couldn't get a ride either to LRE or Electronic City, I would walk to Whelan's Drugstore in the Plainview shopping center. They had less of a selection and their tubes were more expensive but they were close!

I considered Whalen's to be the emergency room, LRE to be my main doctor and Electronic City in Mid-Island Shopping Plaza (Hicksville) to be its associate. I spent so many hours testing and evaluating the tubes from this radio that I wonder if I might have shortened their lifespan through all the test use! I remember trudging through the snow with the brown paper bag clutched to my chest keeping watch for muggers who might try to bereave me of my precious cargo. I think I might have made it a fight to the death!

I would try to keep the tubes warm inside my coat by keeping them close to my body. I was afraid of the sudden change in temperature from the cold to heating them up in the tube tester might cause them to crack. Who could forget the large garbage can sized tube testers that used to grace every hardware, drug and department store. They were usually banished into some cubbyhole or corner and nested there so we mere mortals could ask their mighty Oracles to cure our ills and tell us what tubes should be replaced.

I felt jaded and frustrated when someone else would be praying at "my" alter when I came to offer a sacrifice! I would give them the evil eye and think nasty thoughts about their ancestry and their parent's marital status! I felt that it was my personal tube tester and others had no right in tying it up! I especially despised the older folks, with the reading glasses perched on the end of their nose who talked aloud while following the systematic instructions provided in the pull-out tray. They always took too much time in trying to figure out what they were supposed to do and I had a deadline of the store closing.

I first met Harry this way. I was on one of my "emergency" runs to Whalen's when I noticed an old codger in a frayed gray coat and hat messing with my tube tester. I moved in to reconnoiter. I watched him open the slide-out compartment and try to follow the instructions. He read them aloud. "Hmmm, let's see. First, read off the tube number from the tube that you want to test. Hmmm. I see a 12." Then he would dust it off on his shirt. "Is that a 12Y?" Then he would blow on it as you would to clean your glasses to get water vapor on them. "Hmm, could be a 12YB7. No, maybe it is a 12Y87. Hmmm, could that be a U? Now what was I supposed to do next? Let's see. Find the tube number in the roll chart or spiral-bound book. Hmm. What was that number again? Find the tube socket number 8." He tried vainly to jam the tube in a socket that either wasn't made for that tube or was not aligned properly to the keyway. I wasn't worried that he would damage his tube. I didn't care! All I cared about is that he didn't damage my machine and he got off it! He finally got the tube inserted into a socket and it became really bright for a second or two. He started talking to himself again. "Set the filament selector switch to 'N.' WARNING: Do not plug the tube into this socket before making this adjustment! It could damage this tube! Dadgumit it! There is another bad tube!"

I couldn't stand it any longer! This guy was driving me nuts!

"Excuse me, mister, are you almost done?" I said and interrupted his conversation with himself.

"What say there, young fella? Got some tubes to test, do ya? Well, that shows what this world has very little of now. That's called patience. Hey, when I was a young fella about your age..." My eyes looked like I was following a tennis match as they went back and forth between the wall clock and the number of tubes he had for testing. I knew the store was going to close in less than 15 minutes and I needed to fix a modulation problem with my radio.

"Are you listening to me, son? That's another problem with this younger generation, you don't listen!"

"Well, sir, I just need to know if you will be done soon" (like before I die of old age!)

"Well, sonny, I will be done directly as soon as I finish testing these here tubes." With that, the old geezer whips open a grocery bag with about 100 more tubes inside! I think it was the first time I pondered murder. Who knows what would have happened if there were no witnesses!

I was so frustrated I decided to go to the store manager. He was with a customer so he told me to hang on a minute.

"Now, who is bothering you, son?" He looked around and Harry was the only person left in the store.

"Are you talking about that old codger over at the tube tester? Oh, pay him no mind! That's only Harry! He's harmless! Harry is a little 'touched' and a whole lot lonely. He used to hang out in the store and bother the customers. One day, the previous store manager finally had to tell him to either buy something or leave. Well, someone was testing tubes at that same tube tester when this occurred. Harry pointed to him and said, 'well, look over there, he isn't buying anything!'"

"Yes, but he is testing tubes!"

"Well I gotta test tubes too!"

"So every time a customer throws away his old tubes, old Harry over there picks them up and puts them in his bag. He sometimes tests them all-night until the store closes! He keeps the customers company with his old yarns." That made me determined to smash all my old tubes before throwing them away or at least take them with me! After that, I tried my best to avoid going to that store. I tried planning my monthly tube testing so I could always test my tubes at LRE or Electronic City.

I always looked forward to the weekends. I could spend most of my time in my reality. I would turn the CB on and turn the squelch up so only the locals and my friends would be able to break though. I would listen a lot more than talk until it got later. I used to listen to a radio station that had a show called, "Midnight with Roscoe." Roscoe had a deep, relaxing voice and he was cool and smooth. He never got perturbed and he always provided good advice. That is what I wanted to sound like on the radio.

I was looking forward to a relaxing weekend. I was listening to the radio and finishing my homework so I had the weekend free to indulge in CB radio, when I heard Dan break in.

"Hey, anybody listening, this is the AstroCookie." Dan lived close to me and was a solid 50 db over S9 on my "tight meter." I decided to take a break and indulge. Hey, what do you want, I had a tough week!

"Hey, Dan what are you up to?" I said in a relaxed voice. There was a pregnant pause.

"Hey guys, is anyone out there listening?" He didn't come back to me! I held down the mike and checked my output. I was putting out a little over four watts and my SWR was a tad over 1.2:1.

"Dan, are you copying me?"

"If there is someone trying to get back to me, all I see is a dead carrier with an AC hum. You have no audio! If it's a wise guy then take the pipe!" Oh, no, my "baby" was sick! When I had given my baby her quarterly check-up, her modulation tube was a bit gassy and I was supposed to buy one when I got my allowance more than two weeks ago! I started to panic. I turned up the gain on my Knight Compressor preamp to the max and screamed into the microphone, "Dan, can you hear me? Hey, it's Bob! Hello, testing 1 2 3!"

"I hear a little voice in the background and a big hum. Try it once again and I will turn up my volume all the way."

"Dan, it's me Bob!"

"Bob? Your audio is terrible! You gotta get that thing fixed!" It was too late to visit my normal "doctor" and he didn't make house calls! I had to take my baby to the emergency room before it was too late! I quickly removed the knurled screws that kept the faceplate and chassis attached to the chrome case. I slipped the case off and started pulling all 10 of the tubes out. I had only one-shot at this and I couldn't afford to make a mistake! I grabbed the still hot tubes and they started to burn my fingers. I held on to them rather than let them fall. I packed them with some newspaper then in a paper grocery bag. I ran all the way to Whelan's Drugstore. My face was flushed, and I was out of breath when I got there. I made it with 10 minutes still on the clock before closing! I went to rush over to my tube tester and there he was! It looked like it was one of Harry's nights! I hurried over to the tube tester and I was still out of breath.

"Whoa! Hold on there fella! Where are you going, to a fire?" He said in his crotchety, old voice. I had no time for this! If I didn't get this tube I would be SOL for the weekend's Night Owls club! It would ruin my weekend!

"Look...I ... got... tubes... test...radio... weekend." I couldn't get my breath to get my message across and the hands on the large circular clock on the wall were moving inexorably toward my doom!

"So, you wanna test some tubes? Do you mind if I stay and keeps you company while yer doing it?"

"No... great...I mean yes, keep me company..." All I had was the tube tester as my universe. I had the settings memorized and I didn't have to consult the directions. The store manager gave the 5-minute warning buzzer and turned out the front neon-sign and half of the fluorescent lights. My hands were a blur as they flew across the machine like some mad pianist in the Phantom of the Opera. I pushed slide switches and rotary selector knobs with the deft precision of a surgeon. I was flying on adrenaline. I waited for the modulation tube to heat up and kept jabbing the "test" button. I was treating it like the carnival strong man machine. It was as if I could make the needle climb higher if I hit it hard enough!

Finally, it started coming up slowly and then collapsed. The needle landed firmly in "Replace." I opened the bottom door of the tube tester and started searching for my 12yb7 modulation tube.

"What tube you looking for, sonny, maybe I can help?"

I just about screamed out, "12yb7!" It couldn't be! I couldn't find one among all the RCA, red and gray cardboard tube boxes that had been tidily arranged for size! They were out of stock! It was all for naught! I had beat the clock against all odds and they didn't have the one freaking tube I so desperately needed!

"Did you find what you were looking for, young feller?" I was at the point of boiling over. I didn't have the patience to deal with this!

"OK folks, the store is officially closed. Please bring your items to the cashier or exit by the main entrance." The tears of frustration stared to well in the corners of my eyes. It wasn't fair! I had made it in time! It just wasn't fair! I was into full swing of feeling sorry for myself as I dejectedly trudged toward the exit. I felt a tap on my shoulder and whirled around.

"Did you want these tubes?" It was Harry. He had glommed my bag of tubes that I had left on the tube tester, in my disappointment!

"Give me those!" I yelled and savagely yanked them out of his hands.

"Did you find the 12yb7 tube?" He asked in a small, frail voice. Did I find the 12yb7 tube? Did I find the 12yb7 tube? I turned on him ready to blast him with all my pent up anger and frustration and found him holding out some tubes in his dirty hands.

"I did! I found seven of 'em!" Harry beamed as he held them out to me in his grubby paws. Harry had saved my life! What could I say? The tears ran down my face, I hugged him and I took the tubes I thanked him and walked Harry home. Harry lived alone. He lost his wife seven years ago and he never had any kids. He lived on his modest pension. He played chess! I made a date to play chess with him in the park when the weather got nicer. Sometimes your savior comes wearing the clothes of your enemy. He was a sheep in wolves clothing! I guess that sometimes you have to look past the outer garments to see the real person.

Six out of the seven tubes worked and three out of those six worked well. I don't know whatever happened to Harry but if you are ever stuck behind him in line at that big tube tester in heaven, please be patient and talk to him!

The thing that scares the "bejesus" out of me is except for the arrival of transistors and a family, I could have been Harry now! He was only in his late 50's or early 60's!

In My Room

One of the things I got in trouble for was waking my parents while talking on the CB late at night. Our bedrooms shared a common wall. I went to earphones to help prevent this but they gave me headaches and I still talked too loud, especially when I became excited. The final solution was building a soundproof room in the basement.

My room was in the far right hand side of the basement. It captured two of the small rectangular casement windows that opened up and out because they were hinged at the top. It was a small room, maybe 8' X 7'. It was my "Fortress of Solitude" in one aspect and my gateway to my friends in another. It was where I meditated, medicated, and ah talked to my friends, entertained, listened to music and shut out the world when I wanted to. It had strobe lights and spotlights that pulsed to the music. I had black lights and Day-Glo posters. The room had battleship gray walls, green carpeting, and a dropped ceiling with soundproof ceiling tiles. There wasn't much room to entertain except for one or two besides myself. If there was a party, the door had to be open so it could spill out into the basement. The exception was very private parties of three or less. I had tiger curtains, posters such as "Easy Rider" and Jimmy Hendrix's Day-Glo head.

I had an old solid wood table my grandfather brought over one Sunday. We put a small back lip on it and painted it "battleship" gray. It held my CB radio station a small B &W TV set and my LRE stereo equipment. I can't remember ever acquiring a 40-channel base CB set. The only transistorized base radio that I remember was the LRE SSB-100. It was a beauty and has sideband capability too. I guess I was well into amateur radio or the pursuit of young females when 40-channel radios made their entry into the marketplace. My room came in handy for this other pursuits. It was soundproof and had a locking door! My signal wasn't as good from this location at first, as I had to use a ¼ wave ground plane that was stuck in the hole in the ground the collapsible wash line used to occupy. In this location, I could stay up all-night and be just about as loud as I wanted. I rejoined the Night Owls club with gusto! I now could keep the volume up and make as many comments as I wanted!

Mommy Dearest

One day we were all invited to Ted's house. We stopped there to pick him up and his mother invited us in. We were adults (at least in our own minds!) We drove cars and we were 16 & 17 years old! Ted's mother doted on him. She acted like he was her only child and I knew he had a brother. We were hanging out in his overcrowded, hot room, which smelled of body odor and morning breath. The room also contained his CB radio shack. His mother came in with some cookies. After we indulged, we decided it was time to leave. As Ted got up to leave, his mother started sniffing him like a dog. She stuck her face close to his body and made the "bitter beer face" from a gurning contest when she got to the armpit area. "Ted, you stink!" His face turned a vivid shade of crimson.

"But mom, I gotta go now!

"Young man, you have to take a shower!"

"Well, I'll take one later! We have to go now!"

"You are not going anywhere until you take a shower!" Phew, Phewie! You stink!"

"The guys are waiting for me!"

"I am sure that they don't want to smell your little piggy smell and they are willing to wait 10 minutes for you! Now go!"

We were all embarrassed for Ted and waited for him in his room while he took a shower. We sat there on his bed and discussed the situation. We felt bad for him and wondered how we could make him feel better. There was almost nothing worse than being treated like a little kid by your parents in front of the guys. It put a huge crimp in your "larger than life" radio persona! We were quiet. Some of use were wondering how we would feel if it had happened to us. When he returned, we did our best to console him in true misfit fashion. We mercilessly sniffed him all-night and thought of all the exclamations we could think of to suggest that he smelled! At first, we mimicked his mom and then we became inventive "Phew! Phewie! You stink! Do you have a dead skunk in your pocket or are you just happy to see us?" Well, what do you expect from teenagers, especially misfits?

Going Mobile!

Our first set of "wheels" were bicycles. We used them extensively to get what we needed in the local area. We didn't get carted around as much as kids do today nor would we have wanted to. We didn't have cell phones nor the change to call our friends. We were always within earshot of our radios to keep plugged in on what was happening in our group. We were more independent and being in the presence of our parents didn't allow us to be ourselves. We first used walkie-talkies on bikes but they didn't have the range or the audio we needed. LRE offered some radios designed for special use like the HA-150. It was a 1-watt radio in the mobile style. It had a separate handheld microphone and an internal battery compartment. It also had a telescoping whip antenna. You could use it like a mobile radio in a car or take it with you walking or on a bike and operate like it like a walkie-talkie.

Our final solution was to use a mobile radio, mount a 108" whip antenna to the bike, and provide some source of power. Some used the HB-525 series of mobile radios. Some tried to carry their full weight 11-tube base radio in their baskets. This was a recipe for disaster! The use of the HB-506 adaptor with the HB-525 series of radios was popular. The HB-506 was a D-cell battery adaptor for the HB-525 and HB-625 mobile radios. You could then use either Ni-Cad or Alkaline D-cell batteries to power the radio.

Others preferred the brute force method and carried a car battery in a basket or tied onto the bike. Both the radios (especially one of the big tube radios) and the car battery added weight and made the bike unbalanced. I feel it was the cause of many accidents. It contributed to many bicycle mishaps but none that were life threatening that I know of. But then again, back then, if you got hit by a car, you would try to hide the fact from your parents and deal with the war wounds incurred by yourself! Some of this was because of the fear of punishment. A big part was fear of losing your freedom to bike ride to places like LRE, Electronic City in the mall, Harrison radio and Heath-kit.

As we became old enough to drive, we put CB radios (also known as rigs) in our cars. Before we were old enough to drive, most of us put a rig in our parent's cars and used them when we went along for the ride. However, this usually ended up cramping our talking-style and sometimes kept us off the radio for a while when our parents heard how the other "bad influences" talked over the radio. Sometimes I would "sign-in" and point out that I am here with my father in his car. This in theory would warn the other guys to "keep a lid on" the language. Invariably, someone like Barry would show up after I made the announcement and say something like "Hey guys, why are you talking so funny? Are you shitten me?" You have to remember in those days, there were no four-letter words that existed in front of your parents. You would "get a beating" or your mouth washed out with lye soap if you said something like that. The F-word could bring instant death!

The Night Owl Club

One of our favorite times was talking on the radio late at night on the weekends, while watching television. This was before we had wheels or dates. The wearier we became, the more barriers dropped. As the hours wore on, the built-up layers and masks peeled away like steaming off the many layers of wallpaper on a house built in the 1930s. In the end, all that was left was the raw original structure. It consisted of a lonely, human being looking to share a laugh, a smile, and each other's company. Sometimes it's hard being a loner and sometimes it's best to be alone with your thoughts. Loners unite! You have nothing to lose except solitude!

Being able to share your thoughts and not be encumbered with the "Politically Correct" thinking, fear of ridicule, false bravado, and making a connection to the inner being of another, is a warm feeling. I cherished those moments, as they can never last. I think that is part of what makes them so special. The more you can share these moments with a close friend, the more special it makes that friend. Even when you think that you are having a "private" conversation on CB radio, there was no way of knowing for sure if more people are listening.

The evenings wore on into the night and then into the early hours of the next morning. As the night wore on, members of the group would "sign off" and drop out as fatigue overcame their need for companionship. It usually came down to two people left on the radio but neither wanted to be the first to leave.

I guess these were two of the loneliest of the group. Their inner need for camaraderie overcame their exhaustion and gave them a "second wind." There was also some sense of accomplishment at being able to stay up later than anyone else in the group. I guess it is a male thing that surfaces in competing for dominance and therefore the ability to select and mate with the best females! I guess it was a "survival of the futile!"

There was some common bond that we didn't want to give up. We shared in some unspoken pact of loneliness that we were too proud to admit. I whiled away many late night hours with the Night Owl and Starship. We were an allegiance of misfits that found comfort and security in each other's company through a voice over a speaker. As I write this, it does not sound as comforting as it was. You have to feel the mood to understand it. My room was soundproof and sound deadening. The lights were all off. The room was lit only by the bluish reflections of the black and white TV set and the warm orange glow of the radio tubes. The TV set imposed harsh, weird, moving phantoms on the wall. The radio was warm to the touch, almost like a warm human body. The room had two external casement windows that were covered by heavy material. These hand-made tiger-stripe curtains blocked all vestiges of light. The radio provided the "body" that my friends spoke through. The soundproof room was in dead silence except for the voices and radio sounds emanating from the radio's speaker. The TV set volume was turned low or off.

We sat back in our most comfortable chairs and clutched the "lollipops" of the D104's, the Chrome and iron base of the "Green Hornet" or the small svelte shape of the Turner +2 in our hands. We also rested them on our knees and laps when listening. I think that I entered some altered state of consciousness where everything and everyone else faded out. I was there in my darkened room talking to my only friends and my mind's eye supplied all the rest. Although we only talked to another voice at the other end of another radio, our minds were filled with the rich images and detail of this other reality. We entered this altered state of perception and transcended our miserable earthly existence. We shut out the outside world and entered a world of our own creation. Nothing else existed or mattered. The limited communication quality of the audio, the hums, whines, carriers, heterodynes, interference and adjacent channel splash all helped punctuate the difference of our world. It was our safe haven. We retreated into a world where we were accepted. We portrayed ourselves there as the people we wanted to be and sometimes even became. I guess it was a starting point for us in the coming-of-age process. As we began to know one another, we dropped some of the layers of masks and the male chest pounding and wanted to know what the others thought. We also asked for their insight in navigating the awkward, dangerous, turbulent waters of our adolescent years and in trying to gleam the key to being successful with women, living and society. Some of us even made it!

Channel-10 was a favorite channel in our area. We made it our channel. Then, there were only 23 Normal CB channels. Some time later radios had 22 A & B, which were two additional channels for restricted use. I wasn't allowed to go out even on the weekends and I couldn't have anyone over to our house. I could not use the phone or receive phone calls. My CB radio was my lifeline.

I remember watching old Science Fiction and Horror movies on TV on a Friday and Saturday night. We went well into the wee hours of the next day trading snide comments back and forth with the group of like-minded participants of the "Night Owl Club." As the night wore on, the group would get progressively smaller as some of us signed off, some had to leave, and others fell asleep at the switch.

It was like an early version of Mystery Science Fiction Theater 3000! We would get so tired staying up all-night; we would get slaphappy and silly. We were desperate for some strange kinship. "Night of the Living Dead", "Plan Nine from Outer Space", "Attack of the Crab monsters", "The Crawling Eye", "Forbidden Planet", "The Thing", "This Island Earth," and "Godzilla" movies were some of the late night fare.

The Last Word

As the night moved on past the midnight hour into the early AM hours, the crowd began to lean out as the members of the group "signed-out" or fell asleep. In any case, as the time closed in on the next morning, the comments became sparser. Sometimes 30 minutes to an hour would pass between comments with both parties dozing off and awaking long enough to insert a comment. It turned into a contest of wills to see who could stay up the latest and get to say "the last word." This became a game and at first saying "last word" and waiting for an hour or more just to hear the same. Then it progressed to finally uttering it and turning off the radio in the middle of the sentence so the carrier went down slowly. This was done to show the other party that you turned your radio off so there was no use in continuing the game. The other party could tell you weren't listening anymore so it didn't matter if they volleyed another exchange, or so the theory went. I couldn't prove it at the time but I think the knob was turned right back on again to see if there was a reply, usually, as a covert operation.

We grew up from kids to adolescents to young adults on CB radio. This was the days before Channel-9 was reserved for React and other emergency services. This was before channel-19 became the "Truckers haven." It was a time when there was mostly silence on the CB band and static. It was a magic time. You would have to turn the dial and monitor for a while before hearing any conversation. Once you were accepted as a member of our group you could always go to our frequency (channel-10) and "key-up," insert your call letters (or later just your handle), and get a friendly response. As soon as you came home from school, the radio went on and often stayed on all-night at low volume with the squelch up.

There was also a morning, before school ritual that was followed. That is when you made your plans for lunch and free periods with your buddies. Not all of us went to the same high school. Most of us went to Syosset and some to Jericho and Hicksville. We mostly kept school rivalry out of our world but it crept back in sometimes during the times of the "big" high school games.

There was much boredom in those days before obtaining a driver's license set us free. We didn't have the high-tech gadgets we take for granted today. I had a little green and white record player on which I would play some old 45s that I managed to acquire. Later we purchased cars, 8-track and cassette tape players.

For me, there was little freedom and much loneliness. The only thing that saved my mind was the ability to find a friend with the push of a mike button and the uttering of a couple of words.

6 - LAFAYETTE RADIO ELECTRONICS CORP.

History - According to their catalogs, Lafayette Radio Electronics Corporation has been around a longtime. If you do the math and subtract the number of years, they claim to have been in business, which was 50 years at the time their Golden Jubilee catalog was published, they claim to have been founded in 1921! That is eighty-three years ago and well before my time so I can neither confirm nor deny it! The Golden Jubilee catalog #710 was published in 1971.

The Lafayette Radio Electronics Corp. had mergers with Concord Electronics, Wholesale Radio Service Company and the Radio Wire Television Inc. Company. Their last merger occurred in 1981. See the section titled "The Most often asked Questions about the Lafayette Radio Electronics Corporation (LRE) for details."

I never heard of LRE before 1962. In 1962, Lafayette Radio Electronics opened a main warehouse store on 111 Jericho Turnpike in Syosset. It would be one of the biggest influences on my life. My first two walkie-talkie sets were purchased there. The first set was an EICO kit (see page 240 of catalog 620) that my father purchased for my brother and I for Christmas in 1962. My father did a beautiful job of soldering them but he didn't have the proper tools to align them to make them work properly!

The second set was purchased in early January, when he couldn't get the first set to work! The first working walkie-talkie set were LRE HE-29B's equipped with channel-10 (see page 268 of Catalog 630A) with genuine leather cases, telescoping antennas and a whole lot of fun. My brother and I used to use them to play Space Patrol Rangers. We would sometimes hear other people that sounded like adults talking over our radios. We tried to talk back but they never heard us. Little did I know someday I would be one of them!

Our Places of Worship

Allied Radio (Knight-Kit), Radio Shack, Heath-kit, Gem Electronics, Electronic City, Harrison Radio, Harvey Electronics, Edlies Electronics, Olsen, and the Lafayette Radio Electronics Corp. were the stores or catalogs I frequented. To visit the store, they had to be within bicycle range. LRE in Syosset, Heath-kit in Old Westbury and Electronic City in Mid-Island Plaza in Hicksville were at the limits of my two-wheel range. Allied Radio, and LRE had the best catalogs. Heath-kit catalogs were my next choice. You had to build these items yourself and you needed all the test equipment to align them. The only item I ever built back then was the Knight-kit Compressor preamp model C-577, which I still have today!

My House of Worship

The Lafayette Radio Electronics Corp. (LRE) warehouse store in Syosset was a brick building with a large brick rectangular sign that proclaimed their name. This was the famous Lafayette Radio Electronics Corp. Logo. As you walked into LRE's front door, the ham/CB radio shack was in the front right corner. It wasn't always in this location but this is how I remember it best. Some of the employees had amateur radio licenses. You could talk to Sherman (K2SHU,) Lester (WA2LIC,) Pete (K2LRC,) John (WA2IZB,) Lewis (K2UEI,) Charlie (WA2TFA,) Jack (WA2PHS,) or Eddie (K0YEJ.) They had a LRE Radio QSL card with all of their names and a drawing of the LRE building in the background.

To the left there was the bargain table (also called the junk room!) It was also the place that they would put the podium for the presidential day sales and auctions. Further in the store, to the right, was the stereo equipment including Don's personal favorite playground, the turntables, and phonograph-cartridges. If you went further straight down, you came to the order entry place. This is where you would fill out a pocketbook sized order form (with colored copies.) You would fill in the stock number or numbers, name, price, and you would bring it to counter "B." It was checked, priced, and put in a pneumatic tube where it "whooshed" off to the back warehouse stockroom. You waited and hoped and finally you were paged by your order number. You went to the cashier and paid. You picked up your items at counter "C" and the guard punched your receipt on the way out. If it was unavailable, it came back stamped with the dreaded "OUT OF STOCK" marking in huge red ink. Getting the "Out of Stock" was worse then seeing a big fat "F" in red pencil on your midterm exam. To the left of the Order Entry was the repair center. This is where Dan and I brought back the AC power supply that "damaged" his mobile HB-525 transceiver.

When I went into the LRE's radio-shack, I just couldn't help but turn one of the CB radios to good old channel-10 to see what was happening in my absence. It was my "lifeline" to the rest of my friends. One time Starship was in the radio room. He had turned all the CB radios to channel-10. A refined couple in a suit and dress came in asking about making a purchase of a CB radio for their little Johnny. The salesmen walked them over to show them all the choices. All of the radios were turned to channel-10 from Starships handiwork. At that moment, Dan chose to come on and ask, "What the fuck is going on with you sorry assholes?" Starship reported he never saw a couple back out of a store that fast! They had a look of shock and horror on their faces. In those days you never said or heard anyone use the "F-word" in public. If you (as a kid) were questioned about someone cursing, you had to refer to it as the "F-word" or face the same potential consequences as the perpetrator! Even that reference caused the intake of breaths and the widening of eyes in shock! Adults never heard that language from kids. They would have been smacked in the mouth, even if the adult were not their parents!

I think the salesmen made their best effort to keep the radios off channel-10 after that!

LRE Radio Products I loved and hated!

LOVED

HB444/25A – The "El supreme" tube radio, which I always wanted in those days but I could not afford with the $179.95 price tag. I now have both an HB444/25 and an HB444/25A in my classic CB radio collection.

HB525 (A, B C, D, E, F) mobile radios – The HB-525 was my first mobile CB radio installed in my dad's car (as I did not drive nor did I own a car at the time.) This was both good and bad. It was good that I could talk to my friends while I was being driven to LRE and other places that I went with my father. It was bad when my father heard how we talked to one another if I wasn't able to warn them that I had a parent listening before the talk started! Love that "delta" tune!

LRE Bullet head Crystal microphone – Alias "The Green Hornet." Cast iron case painted green with chromed grille made by Argonne. It cost a mere $3.95 and provided a lot of punch to your audio. It was the poor boys D-104. It was used with the desk-mike stand, which was composed of a base and a stem. It was a hard price and performance combination to beat. There was also a plastic version for $2.95. This was a piece of junk. I don't know if the crystal was the same but the case would not take any abuse.

Vibatrol Preamp - Similar to the Knight C-577, it had pre-amplification and compression It was not manufactured by LRE but sold by them. I never had one of these back in the old days but I have one in my collection now. Mark and a host of others did. It was one of the popular accessories.

HE 20d – An old standby. One of Dan's first radios.

The Comstat 25A – A good reliable radio but it did not have all the charisma, nor did it provide the knob twisting ecstasy, the HB444/25A had. It was the leader until the HB444/25 series made their debut.

SSB - 100/140 – The best transistorized SSB base radio LRE ever made. It had it all. It had beauty, performance, and the (-140) had all 40-channels. There was an easy modification to extend the range far above 40-channels into what we called "hyperspace." It had beautiful, real wood side panels, real wood grain contact paper on the rest of the metal enclosure. It had a brushed aluminum faceplate and sexy red and green LEDs. It was the pinnacle of perfection for LRE's base transistor CB radios.

Dynacom-40 – The "El Macho Grande" of 40 Channel CB walkie-talkies. It had 40-channels and 5-watts output.

The Courier 1M – Although not a LRE product, they sold it. It is in their 1964 yearly catalog on page 276. I have a particular affection towards it as it was my first CB base transceiver and the one that was my closest friend in those hard, lonely years. It had triple conversion, an all-chrome case with more ventilation holes than case and a flat-black, front-panel that Courier was known for. It was a great space heater for the winter months! It was a solid, heavy radio and I miss her! It had a tunable receiver for 23 + frequencies and a crystal transmitter. It typically included channels 1-12 and a position for external crystals. This position connected an external crystal socket where you could plug in crystals for channels 13-23. It looked more like a military radio than a CB but it will always be a beauty in my mind. The original mike was a black hand-mike with a little circular insert that indicated "ECI." A power mike was required to derive reasonable audio from it.

HATED

The Publicom radios

These radios were dubbed (by us) as the "pubic cum" radios! These ugly plastic boxes were an eyesore and made cheaply!

The Comstat 25B

They made an aesthetically pleasing radio (Comstat 25A) into an ugly plastic monstrosity. I know some people liked this radio. If it was your first radio then it is your "beauty." It was always the "beast" to me. It just never had the appeal to me of the original.

Telsat Radios

Crank them out, make them of plastic and make them cheap! I guess you can't stop progress! I know cost is an important factor, especially when the competition is making them cheaper by the dozens!

Things I Liked and Hated about LRE

HATED

OUT-OF-STOCK

I hated the big, fat, red "OUT-OF-STOCK" stamp your order sheet came back with. It was like a death notice. It shattered your dreams and ruined your weekend. It was especially bad when you needed a bunch of stuff to complete a project and they only had some. Did you part with your hard-earned bucks for what they had and wait for the rest or buy something else? It seemed like you always made the wrong choice. If you didn't pick up what they had, next week the other parts would be in stock but the ones you could have bought would be "OUT OF STOCK!" If you purchased the first part the others would never be restocked and you would find something you couldn't afford that you wanted more! Oh, the inhumanity!

THE ELIMINATION OF THE WAREHOUSE STORE

When they changed the Syosset store into a regular store and made the warehouse portion separate. You had to order the items as usual and wait 3 days for them to see if it was in the warehouse just three "farking" feet away from you! Then items were "OUT-OF-STOCK" a lot more often even though you "knew" they were just 3-feet away in the warehouse! This was their version of the Chinese water torture. It indeed was the ultimate cruelty!

LIKED

The Yearly Catalog

LRE's yearly catalog had stuff only dreams were made of! I couldn't wait for each yearly one to come out. I had to make due and used the supplements to feed my addiction until it was time for the real thing to make its appearance.

Tent & Presidential Day sales

You could be "rich" for a dollar and a dream! If you got there early enough or were lucky enough to be standing there when they put out some more goodies at fire sale prices!

The Junk room and discounted returns

There were many items returned to LRE. Some could not be sold as new as some of the parts were missing or the customer said it was "not working properly" or some of the shipping or packing material was missing. Many times, there was nothing wrong with the equipment. Sometimes items were discontinued and no longer stocked. If they were too busy or lazy to test it, or could no longer stock it, it ended up here at greatly discounted prices. It was all a matter of timing. If you were there after they happened to put out a new load of goodies, it was better than winning the lottery! Well at least it seemed that way to us as kids!

I heard stories of some of the group buying things then returning them as defective or missing parts and then waiting at the junk room for them to show up. They were able to get a bargain when they replaced the missing parts!

The Dream Catalog

A favorite "hang-out" of our group was the Lafayette Radio Electronics Corporation. Their yearly catalog was a well-anticipated event. It was our wish list. The person to secure the first edition of the new yearly catalog was in a position of power. He could quote the new CB set models, features, and prices. We would all be envious and he would know and take full advantage of it by tantalizing us with tidbits from the latest catalog over the radio. This would continue until we could make it there and acquire one of our own!

The "pressure" was sometimes too much to bear and it resulted in a mass exodus to LRE. Within a day, everyone was pointing out the wonderful new radios and accessories they liked and which pages they were listed. If you had been so unlucky to be away when this happened, you felt excommunicated from the group! You had no knowledge of what everyone was talking about and no one wanted to talk to you! There was only one solution! You had to head down to LRE as fast as your bicycle pumping legs could carry you! Now, if you were really unlucky, there was a gorging run on the catalogs and they were temporally out of them until the next run came in. Your only hope at this point was that one of your buddies picked up a spare for you. There was one other alternative more on the seedy side. As LRE had limited stock of the catalogs, they were supposed to be one to a customer only. Some of the "wheeler-dealers" glommed as many as the store would allow them to take on multiple visits. Sometimes they wore "disguises" like different hats and scarves so they wouldn't be recognized. They would be glad to sell you a free catalog for as much as the traffic would bear! They would pretend it was their only catalog but they could bear to part with it and wait for the next run if you parted with enough green. They liked to think of themselves as apt businessmen but I have a lot more names for them! I won't mention any names but you guys know who you are!

The LRE Follies

The Ole shell game!

There was an astute observation made by a member of our little group on LRE's return policy. This occurred during a CB conversation early in the morning before school. "You know one thing that is really great about LRE is their return policy. You could always return it if you don't like it." said Dan.

"Ya, you could even return it if you do like it," said Barry

"Barry, why the hell would you return it if you did like it?" demanded Ted.

"Hey Barry, intelligent answer as usual." Dan interjected.

"I'm juusst, just saying that yoouu, you could if you wanted to! That's all," Barry stuttered. Barry often stuttered when he got excited, upset, or was put on the defensive.

"Gee, maybe I will return my Comstat 25A, my D104 and my Collinear because I like them too much," bantered Mark.

"Yep, there goes my HE-20d and my scanner antenna, I really love them, so back they go," added Dan.

"Oh, cut it out guys, I was juusst, just saying that you coo...cooo...could if you wanted to! I didn't say that you hadda!"

"You know you could even beat it to death and then return it on the 30th day. As long as you tell them it works OK, they never even check the box! They put it right back into stock!"

"You could switch it with your old beat-up version of the same radio and keep the brand-new one!"

"Heck, why waste a perfectly good radio! Just give them back a box with a brick in it of the same weight and they will never know the difference," laughed Paul.

Suddenly, there was radio silence except for the buzzing and whining of distant carriers. Pandora's Box had been opened and the idea galvanized us. Everyone's mind was going 60 miles an hour but didn't want to put forth their thoughts on the air, if at all. Who couldn't use a brand-new top-of-the–line LRE CB free! The silence stretched out into infinity.

"Ah, I gotta go, or I'll be late for school!"

"Yeah, me too!" and the avalanche of signoffs started. To my memory, the subject was never discussed again, at least not on the air. A couple of months later I did hear of several instances where parents rewarded their prize progeny with a brand-new LRE CB set only to get a slightly used brick! All this came about from one innocent CB conversation, an exceedingly dumb comment and LRE's no questions asked (except if it was defective) money-back guarantee. Because of the large volume of business and the small number of busy techs, the returned products were not opened or inspected at the time of return. If you indicated it worked fine but you decided you didn't want it anymore, they just restocked it to the warehouse shelves. If you pointed out it was defective, it would wait on a separate pile for the techs to look at it. Someone in our group realized the only feature observable about a returned item, without opening the box, was the weight. He decided to try an experiment and returned a base CB radio box with a concrete brick. It worked! It opened the floodgates for the misuse of this system and I'm sure provided some nasty surprises for some honest hardworking people who found out they just paid $299.95 plus tax for part of a concrete block or brick! I never took "advantage" of their system in this manner as I knew it was wrong and I didn't have the nerves to do it. I think I would have had a heart attack but many must have tried it. I have my suspicions who did but I think I would rather not know for sure. It must have been just a coincidence that Don, Phil and Todd were selling "new" in the box LRE CB's for discount prices!

I thought this wrong back then but now I think it is even worse if it is one of the reasons that led to LRE's ultimate demise. It did result in the hiring of a new company "watchdog" and a major shift in the return policy.

Smoke Test

Dan had a LRE HB-525 mobile rig that didn't work anymore. It was well past the warranty period. It looked like it provided communications for a demolition derby. He wasn't the original owner of the well-used radio. He recently purchased the matching base power supply so he could operate it in the house. He was trying to figure out a way to exchange the nonworking radio for a new one. I suggested that we might make a slight adjustment to the AC power supply he recently purchased. In that way, we could blame the demise of his HB-525 on the power supply and they would fix them both free. At the time, it didn't seem there was anything wrong with this, as it was their radio that had broken! I do not agree with this philosophy today and I am embarrassed that I could even think this was OK to do back then but I did do it. I reverse wired the dc output leads on the connector and replaced the fuse with a piece of #12 awg ground wire cut to fuse size. We boxed up the power supply and the radio and were on our way.

We were unlucky, we got Mr. Harnner. We had been warned about this addition to the company. He was hired to "crack down" on the thefts and allow the company to be more profitable. He was only supposed to be there during the week but for some reason he was there this Saturday. He was tall, thin and bald with a comb over that started at his left ear that glued seven or ten scraggly black strands across his sickly white pate. He had a craggy, pockmarked face from a bad childhood experience with acne, I supposed. He had a hawk nose and close-set, feral, piercing, black eyes. We heard stories about what happened to the kids that he fixed with the glare of those twin black pits that were windows to the darkness of his soul. He had a reedy bird screech of a voice that jangled your nerves and made you jump every time he spoke. He always spoke in jarring, bursts with no rhythm. He always wore a black vest over his white shirt and tie. He had a sour attitude and didn't mind showing it to us brats. "So, what do you guys want now?" He said as he pinned us to the spot with his narrow beady eyes. The both of us began to sweat. "Ah, We would like...ah to exchange this defective ah...power supply and ah...and …mmm, have this radio repaired."

"What do you mean defective power supply? There ain't nothing wrong with that power supply! Yur just trying to get a new radio for free! Give me that!" With that, he snatched the power supply from Dan's grasp like a cobra striking an unsuspecting mouse. He held it in his long bony arms that were stronger than they looked. We felt sick, embarrassed and wanted to crawl under anything we could find. There was a group of people around and they seemed to be all whispering and pointing about us. Mr. Harnner returned with a new HB-625 transceiver and the power supply. "I'm gonna show you kids that there will be no more of that exchange crap around here now that I'm here! You may have gotten away with pulling this kinda junk before, but not on my watch! I fully intend to make an example of you two, to send a message to the rest of your hoodlums! This will let them know that there is no more free ride since Harry J. Harnner Jr. is on-the-job!"

There was a crowd of adults and parents forming. Our faces became hot and crimson from the infusion of blood. If we just could have just taken our radio and power supply back, we would have. "Ah, look mister, I wouldn't... I mean don't put that power supply on. It's defective... I mean..." I never got to finish the sentence.

"I'll bet that you don't want me to turn on this power supply. That's cause there ain't nothing wrong with it and it will show you up for the little lying, conniving, thieves you are! Even if there were something wrong with the power supply, it would blow the fuse and protect the radio!"

This was not going well! I felt like I was going to faint. I had never done anything like this before and I was sorry I had got involved. With that, the store manager appeared. "Harry, what seems to be the problem here?" He said nervously eyeing the two of us and the substantial crowd that was forming.

"Ah, Mr. Finmoore, we have here in front of us today two of the little hoodlums that have been robbing us blind. They tried to pull one of their little swindles on me and I wouldn't go for it!"

"That's it! I'm outta here!" It was time for me to exit stage left! I turned around to lose myself in the crowd then head for the door! Dan wasn't far behind. The boat was sinking and it was children and kids first! "Going somewhere boys?" We felt someone grasp our jackets from behind and haul us back. It was Phil, the stores new rent-a-cop!

"You wouldn't want to miss Mr. Harnner's interesting and informative demonstration, now would you?" The smell of his unwashed uniform, that was worn for several weeks in a row, and bad breath that reeked of tobacco, liverwurst and onions washed over us. It seemed like there was no air left in there! I had to get air!

"Listen Harry, if the kid's radio is broken, let's just replace it and not make such a big deal..."

"Big deal! Big Deal!" Mr. Harnner blurted in escalating tones. "These little ruffians have been destroying store property, stealing radios and returning empty boxes with concrete bricks in them!"

My legs went to rubber underneath me. Just please let me get out of this one! I promise I'll never do it again, I swear! I silently prayed to some unknown deity. Desperate times required desperate measures. I was praying to a supreme being that I didn't even believe in! Well, it couldn't hurt!

"Harry, you actually witnessed them doing all of these things?" For the first time, Mr. Harnner seemed to lose some of his composure. "Well...No Mr. Finmoore, but I know they've been doing it! It's them and a bunch of the other hoodlums from their gang."

"Phil, have you seen these boys pilfer or otherwise remove any property from the building without paying for it or not?"

"Well, no. I mean, no Mr. Finmoore!"

"Harry, I fail to see..."

"Look at this!" Mr. Harnner showed Mr. Finmoore the old beat-up HB-525 and power supply.

"They stole an old beat-up radio?" Mr. Finmoore asked dubiously.

"No, No, No! They wanted to trade this relic for a new radio and claimed that it was our power supply that damaged it! I wasn't about to let them get away with it! I was just about to prove them guilty when you showed up!"

"Well maybe the boys have a point. They look like good boys. Why don't we just give them a new..."

"Watch this Mr. Finmoore." Harry connected the radio to the power supply and turned it on. There was no response. "Oh, I forgot to turn on the power supply!" He flipped the switch with flourish and was rewarded with the transformer hum and the power light. "See! See! I told you! There is nothing wrong with this power supply! It's those damn little bastards over there!" He whirled, and almost danced with glee and began shaking and pointing the finger of doom at us! All eyes were on us. There was the silence of the graveyard. Dan and I looked at each other with shocked, sick expressions on our faces. Dan's face was pasty white. They were going to blame us for everything that had been going on here over the past eight months! I needed air. I was going to be sick. The air was a stale mix of body odor, bad breath, and burning phenolic (a type of plastic used on printed circuit boards). The burning phenolic smell became stronger by the moment! I turned around to see wisps of smoke reaching out its tendrils from the shiny new 626 CB transceiver.

"Look! Look! I told you! I told you!" I frantically pointed to the now dense clouds of acrid smoke that began pouring out of the radio. Everybody's eyes turned toward the radio erupting into flames. Mr. Harnner's mouth was agape. His composure was gone. The crowd was now turning against him! Mr. Harnner couldn't get close enough to the radio to turn it off. The flames were consuming the paint and the plastic faceplate, knobs and dials were melting. I began to hear murmurs in the crowd.

"My kid has one of those at home," said a big guy with a green flannel shirt.

"That could have happened to my little Jimmy," cried a woman in a gray coat.

Another one said, "He called our kids bastards!" They were losing control and the crowd was turning into an ugly mob! Someone came in with a fire extinguisher, put out the mess of flaming paint, and melted plastic. Mr. Finmoore was yelling for attention. The excitement, the tension and the stench of burning plastic and rubber was too much for me. I took that moment to launch my cookies all over the floor, Phil and anyone else who was unlucky enough to be in the line of fire. As oft happens, it started a chain reaction and Dan fired off a barrage that filled in the gaps I had missed. We both fell to the floor holding our stomachs. I heard someone yell something about toxic fumes and the fire department arrived. I was fine once I hit the fresh air and the tension began to ooze away. "How are you boys feeling now?" Dan and I looked at each other and the barest trace of a slight smile crept into our lips. We simultaneously clutched our stomachs and fell back into the stretchers moaning. They took us to the local hospital by ambulance. Dan's parents arrived on the scene first. "Are you all right? What happened? Are you hurt?" We bore the usual parental questions of concern. Then Mr. Finmoore showed up.

"Ah, boys, how are you feeling? I brought something for both of you to make up for some of the problems you had today." He gave us each a new HB-625 with new matching AC power supplies and two $200.00 gift certificates to LRE! We (nor did anyone else) ever see Mr. Harnner nor Phil again. Several years later LRE closed its doors forever and another era in our childhood was shut off forever. It is my fervent hope that our "antics" were neither responsible nor aided in its untimely demise.

Testing One, Two, Three!

Near the back of the LRE Syosset store there was a test counter where radios were set up and tested. One day, when I was in the store, I was watching the test technician as I had a question for him. The test technician was a youthful, good-looking black man.

This technician's countenance graces the cover of the 1975 yearly LRE catalog. He had LRE Stereo Receiver up on one end with the top and bottom covers removed and powered up. He was talking to a beautiful, blonde-haired, young woman and trying to score some points. He was not paying attention to the stereo.

"Uh, Sir?" I said. He kept on talking to the lovely young woman. "Uh excuse me sir," I interjected louder this time.

"Excuse me for just a moment while I take care of this!" He said to the cute blonde. "Can't you see that I am very busy at the moment?" He kept shifting his eyes from us to the cute blonde-haired woman. I think he was afraid she would walk away before he acquired her telephone number.

He started to turn back toward the young thing when I once again spoke. "I just wanted to let you know that your stereo radio is on fire!"

"What?" He said as he turned around and looked at me uncomprehending. I motioned my head toward the radio and he followed my gaze.

"Holy Shit!" He yelled as he ran toward the smoking radio that began to emit a small flame. He unplugged it and then managed to get the fire put out before it got too large. Oh the smell of burning phenolic in the morning!

Sticky Fingers and five-finger discounts

LRE was a great place to check out the new radios and pick up a "deal" at the bargain and closeout counter for returned, damaged or demo models. Don hung out there more often than most of us. He always had to put on a show if he was there with other members of the group. He loved to show how brave he was by stealing everything that wasn't welded into place. He would go to the stereo center and pull out all the plug-in, expensive phonograph cartridges from the tone arms with great flair. I don't think he ever used or sold much of the stuff he stole. It was more important to him to elevate himself to "big-man" status within the group. The management didn't share his enthusiasm and took countermeasures. They used superglue to permanently adhere the cartridge to the tone arm and therefore prevent the thefts. Don came by after their countermeasures and went to pull his normal stunts. He tried to pry one loose, then another. He finally realized what happened. He took it as a personal attack and was infuriated. He retraced his steps through the stereo display section, broke off, and pocketed every tone arm in the place!

The Decline and death of an institution

LRE had been in some grave financial trouble for a while. It declared chapter 11 several times. It restructured itself several of those times except of course the last one. They owed too much money to their creditors and couldn't swing it one more time.

There are several factors that contributed to LRE's decline. The Japanese competition from other importers like Radio Shack® became fierce and they overextended themselves when the Reagan administration cut the legs out from under them. After the original president died, the company started to fall apart in a big way. Some of the things I feel contributed to the collapse were the following:

> **Theft** - Theft was rampant within LRE. I think many kids went to work there to steal and sell their ill-gotten gains. We called it "The Midnight supply." You could put an order in to one of your coconspirators that worked inside and he would put the item in the trash and bring it out to the dumpster behind the store. A confederate on the outside would come by and pick it out of the dumpster at the appointed time. Theft occurred in the store and from outside sources. I am convinced that most of the high-ticket items were stolen from within.

> **Overextension of finances** - I think they opened too many stores too fast to compete with the Radio Shack "Godzilla" and became overextended when the recession hit. They reacted too slowly and thought that they had time to recover and times would get better. They did not.

> **Restructuring** – The new president thought he could remake LRE into the "successful" Radio Shack®

paradigm. He had the stock area closed off and made it into a separate warehouse. They created separate, small, internal stockrooms in each store. He did away with warehouse-stores. Maybe it was to even the playing field and make each store equal. Who wanted to go to a store that hardly had any stock when you could go to a giant "warehouse" store! He did make each store equal, now they all "sucked" equally! The dreaded red "OUT-OF-STOCK" stamp would now adorn almost every order. The most frustrating part was that you just "knew" that it was "in-stock" only a few feet on the other side of the wall in the warehouse. Why would you even go there when you knew you would get the "OUT-OF-STOCK" stamp and it would take 3 days to order it from the warehouse only 3 feet away! Even a senior citizen with a walker could move faster than 1 foot a day!

LRE was a long trip by bicycle and it took a longtime to convince my dad to take a ride in the car there on a weekend. It became too frustrating for me to waste my only trip out, to go there. They never had what you wanted anymore but you could order it and wait three days to see if it came in from the warehouse! In retrospect, maybe they didn't have enough stock to go around. It didn't matter what the reason was, I'd rather take my chances at Radio Shack then waiting for three days to find out that they didn't have a crucial part of the order anyway!

The Most often asked Questions about the Lafayette Radio Electronics Corporation (LRE)

1) Why did it close? See the answer to this question in the chapter entitled "The decline and death of an institution."

2) What was LRE's last Catalog? Well this is a tricky question. The August 1979 was their last yearly catalog. It was silver with a white "LRE" logo and only 172 pages if you count the rear cover. I am not sure about their seasonal and circular type catalogs.

3) Was there a 1978 Yearly catalog? I believe the answer to be no. There were seasonal catalogs but I believe LRE was in or trying to recover from one of its chapter 11 episodes and didn't have the time and money to produce a yearly catalog that year. There was a 1979 yearly catalog.

4) In what catalog did the original president, Abraham Pletman's, photograph appear? Abe's photo was in the 1971 Yearly catalog.

5) How old was LRE when they closed their doors? In 1971 LRE celebrated their "Golden Jubilee" with their 50th year in the business. If they made it to 1981, it would have been their 60th year in the business.

6) I see another company with a similar name on the Internet which sells CB radios and audio equipment. Are they related? No. This company was started in 1946 and it is their family name.

7) In which yearly catalog did the HB444/25B CB radio appear? This is a trick question! The answer is none! It may have made a brief appearance in a seasonal catalog or brochure but was never shown in a yearly catalog.

8) Are there hardcover versions of the yearly catalogs? Each of the stores major salespersons received a hard covered version of each yearly catalog. They are much rarer than the soft covered versions.

9) What were the Call letters of the Syosset amateur radio station? This is a trick question. Several licensed amateur radio operators worked there. Pete's calls were the closest to the company initials. They were "K2LRC." There was also Sherman (K2SHU,) Lester (WA2LIC,) John (WA2IZB,) Lewis (K2UEI,) Charlie (WA2TFA,) Jack (WA2PHS,) and Eddie (K0YEJ.)

10) Did they have QSL cards? Yes, they did and I have one. See the figures at the end. It has the LRE building, sign and the "Lafayette Radio Electronics Corp." title.

11) Were there little pins, tie tacks and other items with the LRE logo? Yes! They were provided in the store for salesperson incentives. I have still yet to acquire any of these.

12) When did the Syosset store open their doors? The Syosset store opened in January 1962.

13) Where was their first store opened? I believe the first store was at 100 Sixth Avenue, New York, N.Y. with the 542 East Fordham Road in Bronx store being the runner-up. The Newark NJ and the Atlanta, GA stores have also been around since at least 1935.

14) What was Concord and Wholesale Radio Service Co. Inc.? It is my understanding that these companies were purchased or merged with LRE from the pressure for continual expansion, which aided in their success, and lead to their eventual downfall.

15) My buddy has a 1970 yearly catalog with over 500 pages. I bought on Ebay® and got only 40 something pages. What gives? I have copies of both of these catalogs. Apparently, they copied some of the pages from the 1970 yearly catalog, including the exact cover with the "catalog 700" marking and the year "1970" indicated. They made a full color advertising circular catalog out of them with an extra one-sheet B&W "Last Minute specials" addition. If you want this version, make sure you get this part too! You have to be careful when purchasing one of these as you may think you are getting the real yearly catalog and you get the "wimpy" advertising circular, version instead!

16) What happened to the Lafayette stores and their inventory?

First a little history. In 1949 Samuel S. Wurtzel opened the first Wards retail store in Richmond Virginia.

In 1974 he began opening nine Dixie Hi-Fi "warehouse" audio stores and began closing the original concept Wards stores. He began opening the new "Ward's Loading Dock" stores. They had a large warehouse showroom that displayed a huge selection of appliances, and audio and video items that were sold at retail prices.

In 1977 he began replacing the Dixie Hi-Fi and Custom Hi-Fi discount stores with new-concept "Circuit City" stores.

In 1981 they merged with Lafayette Radio Electronics Corp. and took over eight consumer electronics stores in the New York Metropolitan area.

In 1984 they changed their stores name to "Circuit City Stores Inc."

In 1986 all of the Lafayette departments were closed. All of the resources went to building Circuit City Superstores.

7 - The Games we Played

Hang 'Em High

It was the time of "pirate radio stations" and someone (maybe Todd) came up with the idea of creating our own Pirate radio station. He conned people into "donating" money to buy an army surplus ARC-5 transmitter that he would modify into an AM commercial radio band transmitter. Then we would all take the turns at being the announcer and providing the broadcasting content. To this day, "Pump Up the Volume" is one of my favorite films. "Late night with Roscoe," was one of my favorite radio shows. I liked the thought of being able to express the "real stuff" that goes on inside verses the normal every day banter. We got into that mode on late Friday and Saturday nights. It is during those times I felt the closest to my "friends." During these times, all the "bullshit" petered out and we began to discuss the important stuff on in our minds.

Todd had a way of always amazing me by the displaying his great technical inaptitude. He once took a perfectly good working Knight-Kit CB radio and mounted all the dials and meters on wood paneling to create a "rats-nest" maze of wires and worthless junk. His intent was to create a more expensive-looking, elegant CB set. He didn't know the adding of uncontrolled lengths of unshielded wires to frequency-sensitive circuits, detuned them. I purchased this "hunk-of-Junk" from him for the nominal price of $5.00 and re-created a working CB which I used as my alternate radio for many years.

Anyway, this technical genius was going to modify an old army surplus transmitter (ARC-5 transmitter) to become the pirate station of the area (and get social acceptance, recognition and more important, girls we all secretly hoped!) I was one of the few that didn't ante up and lose my $20.00. It was not that I didn't want to be a part of a pirate radio station; it was more that I didn't believe anyone had the technical expertise to make it happen and Todd least of all! It became a sore point with most of the guys who wanted to take out their $20.00 by seeing if Todd's head was a twist off or a pop-top!

This frustration peaked one day when the guys were venting their feelings toward Todd on channel-10. They found out that Todd's parents were going out for dinner and a movie that evening. A group of nice kids suddenly turned into an ugly lynch mob. I could almost see them foaming at the mouth in my mind! They grabbed a long, car towing rope, made a noose on one end, and headed for Todd's house. They knew his parents wouldn't be back for several hours and it was time for Todd to pay for taking their money and giving them nothing back in return except for excuses.

They had the least threatening member of the mob ring the doorbell while the rest of them hid in the bushes and around the sides of the house. Once Todd opened the door wide enough to admit Ted, they all surged past the door and were into the house.

"Hey, you can't come in here" Todd lamely stammered.

"Hey maybe you didn't notice but we are here already!" Don said in a wicked voice.

"Hey, you guys! You can't wear your shoes on the carpeting! My mother is gonna kill me!"

"Oh, do you mean we shouldn't walk all over the carpeting with our dirty shoes like this!" A line formed and every one started wiping their shoes on the carpeting. Of course Don was at the head of the line.

"Stop it! Stop it! My mother is gonna kill me!"

"Don't you think that is gonna be the least of your troubles? Do you really think we are even gonna give your mother that chance?" Barry said with an ugly sneer.

"Wha...what do you mean?" The look of fear for his person was starting to sink in. This also was the queue to the rest of the guys to try to join in on the fun in terrorizing Todd.

"You didn't think we were just going to take stealing our money lying down, did you?" Don said screwing his face up in a grimace.

"But...but we all agreed!" Todd said in a pleading whinny tone.

"Nobody agreed for you to steal our money!"

"Hey wait a minute, how many of you guys gave this shithead $20 bucks?" Don asked.

About seven guys sheepishly raised there hands.

Suddenly something seemed to dawn on some of the faces.

"Wait a minute, how much did the fucking transmitter cost anyway?"

"Well we saw an ad in the amateur radio paper for $19.99"

"$19.99! Holy fuck! Where did the other $120.00 go?"

Everyone's head turned toward Todd, as if they were on gimbals following the sun. Only in this case, it wasn't a shining star they were facing. He was more like a wilting weed.

"What did you do with our money Todd?"

"Yeah where the fuck is it?"

"Aaaa, I ...I had expenses!"

"Expenses my fucking ass!" Don retorted.

"I say we search his room and find our money!"

Don lead the charge up the staircase and the mob followed.

There were a couple of opened boxes of new stuff on Todd's floor. Don dug right in and started opening up the boxes and checking the contents.

"Hey look he's got a new turntable!"

"Yeah with the most expensive Pickering cartridge!"

Suddenly a look came over their eyes and they looked at one another and realized that they were all thinking the same thing!"

"First dibs!" shouted Don

"Second dibs!" shouted Dan

Then everyone was shouting "dibs!"

They began grabbing everything that wasn't nailed down and putting things in the supplied boxes and making their own "treasure boxes." When the rest of the guys got upstairs it was "slim pickens." Don got the turntable with the new cartridge and stuffed his box with the best of the small goodies. He always made out best when "skullduggery" was involved.

The parade started down the stairs when they heard Todd whining.

"Stop it, you're choking me!"

Barry went too far, as he was prone to. He had the noose around Todd's neck and he was trying to pull Todd around the room with it.

"Come on guys! Tie the other end to the car! Let's hang him and drag him through the streets!" Barry was letting his emotions get out of control once again. He felt like he was in charge and providing wonderful ideas. Nevertheless, some of the guys "played" along.

"Yeah, then what are we gonna due with his bloody carcass afterwards? I am not putting him in my garage freezer! It would stink everything up!" Dan jibed.

"I'm not burying him in my backyard! My mother would kill me when all the flowers and the grass died!" Don added.

"I'm not using my dad's new 7-1/2" table saw to cut up the body either!" interjected another.

"Count me out too! I'm not cleaning my dad's chainsaw afterwards!" Dan added. There was a contest to see who could be the most witty and grisly at the same time. Todd looked like a deer caught in the headlights and was sobbing in shock in the corner.

While they were rubbing it in Barry saw all of the "spoils of war" and ran up into Todd's bedroom to make his own "goodie bag." He re-appeared at the head of the stairs with something in his hands.

"Hey guys, all the good stuffs gone! Who is gonna share with me! The only thing left is this fucking transmitter!" The thing he held in his hands was the ARC-5 transmitter that started this whole mess. We turned to look at it and then one another and then smiled. Barry must have misinterpreted our looks and thought that we had missed it and it was worth something.

"Ah, first dibs?" Barry tentatively called out from the top of the stairs uncertainly.

Todd was all blotchy faced on the floor and he had been crying.

Dan finally went over and removed the noose from Todd's neck. His neck was bright red and raw from the rough hemp rope. Todd began rubbing it and trying to stifle his sobs.

"Hey Barry, bring that down over here so we can look at it for a minute." Dan said with a twinkle of devilment in his eyes.

"What you wanna see it for? It's mine now! I called first dibs!"

"Nobody is gonna take it from you, Barry! I just want to see it for a minute." Meanwhile everyone else had loaded their "ill-gotten gains" into the cars and Dan whispered something into Don's ear that perked him up and made him grin an evil smile. He ran out of the house.

Barry knew something was up but he couldn't figure out what. He started to trudge down the stairs.

"It mine… right? I called first dibs… right?"

"Nobody wants it Barry. It is yours to keep. Just bring it over here for a second and let me see something." Dan said in a calming voice he was known for.

Barry came down and placed it by the front door and Dan started looking it over and adjusting some switches and knobs and making harrumphing noises.

"Is there something wrong with it?" Barry said looking concerned.

"No, I am just trying to figure out something," Dan said seemingly absorbed in his task.

"Hey Barry, can you come out here and help me with this a second?" Don's gruff voice came from outside.

"I'm kinda busy right now!" He yelled back.

"Barry, I thought that you wanted to be helpful and part of our group!" Don replied.

"Go Barry, I'll be right behind you once I figure this out!" Dan told him.

"Oh, Okay, but don't forget to make sure you bring it because it's mine. I called first dibs you know!" Barry said grudgingly.

"Yes, I know Barry. Believe me! I swear that we will bring it with us, OK?"

"Barry, hurry up!" Don's voice cane once more.

Barry started walking towards the door, paused and looked over his shoulder and started to say something when Dan cut him short.

"It is all yours and I will be personally responsible to make sure that follows us home! Now go!" He commanded and pointed toward the door. Barry left reluctantly. Then things started happening fast after that. Dan heard some yelling from outside. "They're home!" All the car engines started up and were revving to warm them up quickly.

Dan looked out the door and saw headlights coming down the block.

Dan ran out and jumped in his car. Barry didn't have a car that he could borrow yet so he rode there in Don's car. The cars began peeling out on the street. Don's was in the driveway facing outwards. "Hey, how come you are in the driveway now and you backed in? You were in the street before and…" Barry said in his confused state of mind.

"I am in the driveway because I know you are so fucking slow and if you don't get in the car now and stop asking stupid-ass questions, I am gonna leave your sorry ass on the payment!"

"Okay, Okay don't get so mad, I was just asking…" Barry was saying as he entered the passenger seat and was interrupted and pushed back into the seat as Don floored it. "Hey wait, I'm not even in the seat yet! Wait a minute!" Barry whined.

Don burned a nice patch of rubber with his dad's GTO. The caravan was off. "Hey Barry, hide your face so they can't see you!" Don cautioned him. Barry was short and hunched himself down in his seat so Todd's parents wouldn't recognize him. As they flew past the approaching car, Barry peered over the doorframe.

"That doesn't look like Todd's father's car. It looks like…"

Don interrupted him and started pushing Barry's head down with his right hand.

"What are you crazy? That's a rental car, their other car is… it's in the shop for repairs! His dad was looking right out you! I hope for your sake he didn't recognize you!"

"Oh shit! Do you think he saw me? I only peeked a little bit. Do you think he knows who I am?" Barry said with his eyes bugging out in a worried tone.

"I don't know, stay down until it is safe!"

Then Don turned on his LRE HB-625 CB radio.

"…bet he shit a brick!"

"Nooo, at least two bricks!"

"Don grabbed the mike "Hey guys, I think they almost saw Barry peeking out the window!"

"I told him to stop smoking or it would stunt his growth"

"Didn't you bring his booster seat for him?"

"Naw I couldn't, my 3-year old sister was using it!"

"What about all those telephone books?"

Barry grabbed the mike and tried to change the subject of his "height" or lack there of.

"I bet Todd's gonna get it! His father's face looked pissed!"

"You saw his father's face?"

"Yep I leaned up just enough to see it without being seen like one of those ninjas and he looked really pissed!"

"Bruce Lee, move over! It's the midget Ninja!"

"Do what he says or he'll kick you in the shins!"

"No, he'll bite your ankles!"

Laughter ensued after each of the quips.

"Hey wait a minute guys! Dan, did you bring the radio?" Barry asked.

"It's right behind you!"

"No, I know you are behind us but where is the radio?"

"Like I said, it's right behind you!"

Barry turned around and looked out the rear window.

"Hey, we're dragging something and sparks and metal parts are flying off everywhere!" Barry stated in excitement.

"I told you I would make sure it came with us!" Dan exclaimed

"I bet it works better now!" Somebody interjected on the radio.

"Didn't someone say that we had to grind the crystals to bring the frequency up?"

"I think a couple of miles more and the frequency will be in the FM band!"

"Guys, that's not funny! Dan, you got the radio in your car, right? You're just kidding me, right?"

"Hey Barry, I only promised you that it would be all yours and I would make sure it followed us home! I kept my promise! It's all yours for the keeping and it is following you home!" Laughter erupted.

"By the way Barry, Todd's father says "hello" he saw a mutant ninja peeking over the car door! He was in the car that looked a lot like Starship's car! Todd's father looks just like Starship, didn't he?"

They put the "head" of the ARC-5 into the noose and tied it to the bumper of Don's car. They dragged it back and forth through town "broadcasting" the event on good ole CB radio. They did this for the benefit of others of our group that weren't fortunate enough to be in the caravan of cars that formed to follow this impromptu lynching and riding "outta town on a rail."

We Be Jammin' Mon!

We were mostly preteen and teenagers. We were all childish. CB radio sometimes brought out the best and sometimes the worst out of us. You couldn't harm anyone except with the power of your words (and curses!) If you were at a loss for words, you could always try to "jam" the frequencies. You could always just depress the microphone button and "throw a dead carrier" on the frequency. If your signal were strong enough, it would interfere with the conversation in progress and disrupt all attempts at communication on that frequency. If that didn't satisfy your element of personal risk and the need for a trademark jamming technique, there were many other methods to choose from. You could disguise your voice, play clips of music, and make noises, most of which were rude. "Nin, nin, nin, nin, nin" said in a deep, gruff voice was always an enduring favorite!)

Certain of us, who loved to jam, would always be on the lookout for little clips of music that would suggest our emotions without having to utter a word. Some of these clips became our calling cards. Circus calliope music was the calling card of one of our friends. He had no need to indicate he was "monitoring" or listening to the frequency. He would just key-up the microphone and you would hear the circus music playing in the background. You then knew he was listening.

Others liked to keep snippets of conversation on tape so you would get insulted or rebuffed by the voice of Mr. Spock or Captain Kirk! It was a hard thing to do in those days as there was no CD-ROM or computer hard drive to play back the right sound file you needed. You had to record them on serial, linear cassette tape or reel-to-reel tape and catalog the clips to the tape counter. Then you had to try to queue them up in time to be relevant. Mark was a master at this particular technique. His timing was superb and his technique, flawless. He was critical to make sure whatever he played came across clear and loud enough but never over-modulated or distorted. He also recorded many CB conversations off the air, which he still has in his archives. He also used snippets from these conversations to fool people into thinking they were being insulted or rebuked by someone else. This was a lot harder back then when you had to record on a cassette tape and index the snippets against the highly inaccurate tape counter. He was a good mischief-maker and still is! It went something like this:

"Hey, anyone around?" Seemingly coming from Dan but just a recording of Dan's voice.

Barry would key up and say. "Hey, what's new and exciting?"

Dan's voice would seemingly say. "Your momma! Well except she's not so new or exciting!"

"Hey Dan, that's not nice!"

"OK, I am only kidding. So what's up?"

"I got a new radio! How do I sound?"

"Why don't you get rid of that piece of junk and get a good radio?"

"This is a good radio! It's the best LRE makes!"

"Your audio sounds like shit and there's a big hum on it!"

"Aw c'mon. It's a new radio!"

"You had better check all of your radio connections"

"OK, I'll check them all-out and check back after dinner!"

The stage was now set. Everyone who was listening before dinner would now wolf-down their food so they could rejoin the game afterwards.

"Hey AstroCookie, are you back yet?"

This time the real AstroCookie responded.

"Hey Barry, what's new and exciting?"

"Your momma but then again she is not new or very exciting!" Barry said with a chuckle and satisfaction. He had outwitted Dan at his own game, or so he thought.

"What the hell wrong with you? Are you on drugs?"

"No, I was just getting even."

"Even for what? Did you steal the cat's catnip?"

"For what you said about my momma."

"Your momma? I haven't seen her in a longtime. I guess it's been since I have been saving for a new radio. I haven't had the $1.50 extra to spare!"

"Hey cut it out! I was just getting even! Now stop it! Barry whined.

"Hey Dan, don't say that about Barry's mother! Besides, she's charging $1.75 because of inflation!" Starship interjected.

"Knock if off guys! I just wanted to know how my new radio sounds!" Barry pleaded.

"I'll make you an even trade for two discount tickets to BJ's" Dan quipped. Barry struck the bait totally unawares and fell right into the trap.

"BJ's? Where's BJ's?" Barry said sounding confused.

The radio audio became clogged with carrier whines and noise as everyone who had a great response to the set-up wanted to get their two cents in. Dan's response overrode everyone else's, at least at my house.

"BJs at your mamma's house! Tuesdays and Thursdays are buy one, get one free nights!"

"Cut it out right now or I am leaving!"

"Cut it out Dan, you know as well as I do the Tuesdays & Thursdays are "all she can eat nights!" Quipped another.

"One more comment and I am turning my radio off! I mean it this time!"

Unfortunately, for Barry, that was just the kind of comment that spurred everyone on and the channel was out of control for at least the next 45-minutes to an hour. Everyone tried to unload their "witty" comments on the airwaves at the target Barry had unwittingly presented.

Barry either left or stayed quiet. Once something like this started, you had to let it settle down and be forgotten unless you had the verbal skills to confront it head-on. Barry was the least capable at quick retorts and most capable of sticking his foot in his mouth and making it a whole lot worse.

As I read this over, I am saddened. In some ways, we were no better than the elite snobs that used the "caste" system at school. Most of us could handle a mock put-down session all in good, clean fun. It wasn't very pretty when it got out of hand and went way too far. I think everyone involved and even just listening were embarrassed and ashamed. We treated Barry nicely for the next couple of days or at least until the next time.

"Watch me scare dis guy!"

Most of the antics that occurred were spontaneous and either for joke value or for status in the group. There was not much forethought about possible consequences. We were less sophisticated kids looking to alleviate the boredom of one day stretching and blending into the next. We had little money and not as many choices as kids do nowadays. We were also testing our wings and the limits of our freedom. There was also a bit of posturing and trying to gain dominance within the group. Heck, if everyone in the group thought we were great, then I guess we could believe ourselves!

I believe that with most or even all of our antics, there was little intent to hurt involved. Although, sometimes things got out of hand, especially when the group started gaining driver's licenses and using them! On reflecting, it is surprising that nobody was killed or severely injured. It was the age of show-offs and muscle cars.

A car was the latest status symbol, entrance into adulthood and deadly toy. Patching out, 360-degree skids, racing and cutting people off were all in the venue. Don was one of the earliest licensed ones. He had his parents GTO and he liked racing it along a local four-lane road (appropriately named Broadway.) Broadway had two lanes in either direction with no divider. He loved showing off. He had a friend in the car and was on the air. He was tooling along when a Senior Citizen pulled out about 30 yards in front of him doing a stately speed of 15 Mph. His classic words shall be forever emblazoned in our minds as he uttered them over CB radio. "Watch me scare this dis guy!" Don then dropped the car into neutral, revved the engine up high and popped the clutch. It made a god-awful roar and screech of tires heard by most of us without the benefit of the radio! Well, the poor old geezer in front of them heard it too. He reacted comparatively swiftly for a gentleman of his advanced age. He slammed on the brakes as hard as his little frame could muster. I'm not sure if I heard or imagined the words of impending doom, "Aww, Shit!" But we could hear the classic screech of tires being asked to do more than they were designed to do and the crash, groan and tinkle of metal, molding and glass meeting their final resting place then nothing but static. In those days, seat belts were optional and experimental. A Lap belt was provided on some of the newer models. I think Don and Dan make their impressions on glass and got slight concussions and cuts but were otherwise unharmed. The GTO was totaled and Don's smooth talking convinced the senior, that it was completely his fault!

"Heh, heh, heh Corvette!"

Barry was the kind of guy that always got under everybody's skin. He was a misfit (even for our little group) and I think he tried too hard to fit in or be cool. He became the butt of many jokes. In retrospect, I feel bad about this but I can't change the past. One night Barry was being more obnoxious than normal. Somehow, there was an unspoken consensus he was overdue for being taken down a couple of notches. His parents went out to dinner and he was home alone. The stage was set! We started talking about robberies and killings that were supposedly happening in the area. Barry started to get edgy and said, "Guys, cut it out!" Of course, this was our cue to continue with gusto! While we kept Barry busy on the radio, Dan drove over to his house. He parked his car down the street where it wouldn't be spotted. He waited until Barry keyed-up the microphone and started to bang on the front door. Barry would get off the radio to see who it was and Dan would hide in the bushes. Then he ran around the back and started scratching on the air conditioner. Barry's voice would tremble as he said, "Cut it out guys! I know it's you guys, so stop-it!" This, of course, always had the opposite effect! We kept egging him on to open the back door and find out who was out there. Then we dared him and called him chicken. At the same time Dan was listening to all this with his walkie-talkie outfitted with a miniature earphone.

Finally, Barry agreed to "check it out." He also agreed to leave his microphone toggled-on so we could hear what was happening. He went to the back door and weakly stuttered, "Who... Who's out there?" There was no response. "Stop it! I'm not kidding. I have a gun!" All of us froze. We had forgotten that Barry's father had a large gun collection! We knew Dan was hiding in the bushes. Then we heard Barry scream, "Come out, or I'll shoot!"

For the first time the possible consequences of our actions hit us like the Titanic striking that "small" iceberg. How could we have been so blind not to see the possible outcomes that were hidden underneath the waterline! We heard Barry go out the back door and scream, and then we heard the sharp retort of gunfire. There were too many gunshots to count. We were all galvanized. Our pulse beat in our eyes. We didn't know what to do. Should we call the police or an ambulance? The seconds turned into minutes that dragged out until eternity. Finally, we heard the door open and slam shut. We heard someone shuffling, stumbling back to the radio. Frustratingly, the very same method that enabled us to hear the whole encounter now prevented us from questioning Barry. His microphone was still open! We heard him yelling to himself and fumbling around. "My eyes! I can't see! Oh, My eyes!" We heard him moan. There was a banging sound as he accidentally hit the microphone and it fell to the floor. Then silence. There was no more carrier.

"Hey AstroCookie!, are you there?" We started calling Dan. Then we called Barry, still no response. We were all there on frequency but nobody could voice what was going on in their head. It was as if we were all connected and an electric current was passing through us. All we could force ourselves to do is call for Dan and Barry. Finally, someone was inspired with a bright idea and called Barry's house. Barry had called the police! Barry finally came back on the air. "That wasn't nice! You broke the back window!" The noise was the sound of several M80 Firecrackers going off in rapid succession on Barry's air-conditioner! The bright flares left their afterimages on Barry's dark acclimatized retinas.

Space: The final Frontier and we are the voyagers...

When Star Trek was first advertised as coming in the fall, it stirred much excitement and talk among the channel-10 crowd. I remember one night in particular that we had a roundtable discussion going on and we were using science fiction and space terminology to create fake and funny "Handles." We were using Spaceship-this, Laser, Ultra and Astro that. What started out as a joke later turned into the handles "AstroCookie" and "StarShip."

I often think back to those days of easy friendship and always having someone to talk to with a couple of key-ups of a microphone. They were magical times that make me feel lonely and sometime wish I were back there when life was simpler. You can never go back, can you?

Radio Persona Non-grada

Static, noise, carrier whines, alternator whines, ignition noise, power supply hums, tinny audio, machismo over-modulated audio all were part of the CB mystique. Carrier whines are created when two (or more) people "keyed" up their microphones at the same time but did not speak. Each transmitter frequency, while being within tolerance, was just a slight bit higher or lower in frequency than the other. When that frequency difference was in the CB audible range (approximately 100 –3500 Hz range), you would hear the tone it generated. This is the basic heterodyning principle. It is also known as the beat-frequency principle. When you mix two frequencies together, you get each individual frequency, their sum, and their difference. The difference created the audio whine we heard.

Basic radios didn't cut it for transmitted audio. They needed help of some kind. A separate pre-amp or a pre-amplified microphone was used for this purpose. LRE tried to cash-in on this by providing their radios with the patented "Range Boost" circuitry. It did work a little better than normal but not enough to give you that big sound-distinguishing quality. The thing I remember most of Don on the radio was his testing of his preamps. It was like the search for the Holy Grail for him. "How do I sound from now 1 2 3" CLUNK "to NOW! 1 2 3! Don was forever testing and improving his 1 transistor preamp.

There is an old theory about making something as simple as possible but not simpler. This also carried over to making something as cheap as possible. How this was applied to electronics was that you took a circuit and kept removing parts to see if it still worked. As long as it still seemed to work, you would remove another component until you got to the point of degraded performance or complete failure to operate.

Well, Don was always testing his preamps on the air. He took a multiple stage preamp design, reduced it to one stage by removing components, and then kept switching the value of the components (and the part numbers of the transistors) to achieve maximum audio amplification power. He did this with while also trying to minimize the number of parts. He created the one transistor wonder that gave thunderous power to his audio on any channel he spoke on (and that splashed over to almost every other one too!) Splashing is a non-technical term for over-modulating your AM signal such that you intrude on other channels (frequencies) in the CB domain. He even began to sell the 1-transistor preamp to other CBers. He rubbed the numbers off the transistor so people couldn't build one of their own. He also kept a special dual-stage version (he connected the output of one into the input of another) for himself so no one could have louder audio than his. It was like having the best of both worlds. He sold his preamp and made money but he still had the best audio with the 2-tranisitor advanced model. Don was a real expert at that!

8 - Was the measure of a man related to the size of his CB station?

Back in those days, it was all-important how you sounded over the CB radio. Listeners could only judge you by your voice. The tone, loudness (your signal strength also played a part in this), and the confidence of your voice was the only things you could project over the radio. They were they only things that could distinguish you from the rest! The stock audio from a CB radio did not distinguish you. You needed something more. Many wealthy kids bought amplified, chrome D104 (lollipop) microphones. I looked for a more cost-effective solution. The D104 was a high output crystal microphone. It came in versions with or without a preamp. The version with the preamp had a hole on the bottom so you could put a screwdriver in and adjust the audio volume control. I always found that arrangement inconvenient. When I finally acquired one of these microphones, I drilled a hole in the top of the base and put in my own volume control.

Before I picked up a used D104, I needed the economy version. I heard of a microphone called the "Green Hornet." I heard it could be purchased at the Lafayette Radio Electronics Corp. store! I grabbed my catalogs and hunted for it. I couldn't find anything called "The Green Hornet." I made some calls on the CB radio and found out the "Green Hornet" was its popular name. It was an "Argonne bullet-head crystal microphone." I had seen that one in the catalog! I bought a LRE Green hornet mike (Part number PA-24 for $3.95 on page 266 of the LRE 1962 yearly Catalog) and a dark gray cast base with a chrome pipe that would be the stand. The stand was part number MA-24 (for $2.94) on page 269 of the same LRE catalog.

I bought all the parts and started putting together my microphone "kit." I drilled a hole in the pipe and fed the "hot" and shielded cable microphone wires down to the base. I made another ¼-inch hole in the base stand and inserted a double-pole, double-throw, bat-handled toggle switch in from the bottom of the base. This acted as the push-to-talk switch for the radio. The center position of the toggle switch put the transceiver in the receive mode. One way was momentary "on" and the other way was latched "on." I made one more hole and inserted the other end of the coiled-cord that plugged into the CB set, so I could wire it to the microphone element and the toggle switch. I used a black rubber grommet around it to prevent chaffing of the cord and present a nicer, more finished appearance. The completed microphone looked every bit as impressive (at least to me) as the expensive D-104 mike.

The "Green Hornet" used a high-output crystal element (like the D-104) that was much better than stock audio but it still wasn't good enough. Shortly after this, I purchased the Knight-kit C-577 Compressor preamp. It was $29.99 assembled and tested or $19.95 if you built it yourself. I bought it in kit form to save money. When I assembled that kit, I treated it with the same care as if I were making a part that went into the Lunar-Lander. I formed the leads to every resistor and diode with needle-nose pliers so the components fit neatly in the holes provided on the printed circuit board (PCB.) I "borrowed" my dad's soldering iron to solder these parts to the PCB. After I built the Knight Compressor preamp I found out that, I still wasn't done! I had to find out someway of connecting it between my microphone and the radio! I was annoyed. It was not like me to be as patient as I had been building the darn thing. I wanted it to work now!

The C-577 had a gray duplex wire coming out of it. Each of the wires had an insulated wire and a shield. One pair was for the mike input the other was for the radio microphone input. Part of me wanted to hack the microphone coiled cord and wire the thing up just to see if it would work and make it "pretty" later. The thing is I knew myself too well. Later would never come and I would become annoyed looking at the abortion every time I used it. I finally sucked it up and became determined to do it right. I drilled one last hole into the gray hammer-tone, mike-stand base and inserted a 3-wire ¼-inch phone jack. I reconfigured the wiring so the microphone element went to the input of the preamp (through the ¼-inch phone jack and plug) and the output went to where the microphone element formerly went. This worked great! It made my voice loud and gave me the ability to toggle the microphone on and, with the compressor knob turned up, roam around the room and even down the hall and still be heard! There were no "roaming" charges in those days! I was ecstatic (not Astatic, which was the manufacturer of the D-104 microphones!) This was my first time attempting this kind of project and I had pulled it off without a hitch! I was very pleased with myself for making it work and look like a professional job! I was also pleased to project the "big sound" on a tight budget!

There was no bottom on the base of the microphone and I liked to hold the stand on my lap with my hand under it. I learned (the hard way!) The old tube radios liked to switch B+ high-voltage on the microphone! Zap! Yikes! The toggle switch I had installed into the mike stand had long, screw-type connectors. They extended a little past the bottom of the microphone and were live! They must have had at least 300 volts on them! A couple of strips of electrical tape later and all was safe, well, close enough for government work anyway!

Dan (AstroCookie)

Dan had a LRE HE-20D, then a LRE HB525C and two stacked 3-element beams that I remember always coming down when we had a windstorm. Finally, after the stacked 3-elements gave up the ghost, he installed an Astroplane. This was one of the weirdest looking CB antennas I have ever seen. I am not sure if it even makes good sense as an antenna design. It looked like a giant lampshade (minus the cloth) that had a wind-speed anemometer (minus the cups) attached to the top with a small mast. He also had various multi-element antennas at different times.

Mark (Starship)

Mark had a LRE Comstat 25 and a LRE Range boost II antenna. This radio had the standard 23-channels as well as 22A & B. Finally, he had a Collinear II antenna, a Kris 200B linear amplifier, a Green Hornet microphone, a Vibratrol preamp, and a "rare" dual-stage Air Raider preamp at the same time. I think he has recreated the entire station except for the mysterious, 2-transistor, Air Raider preamp!

(Bob-Me) The Survivor

I had a Courier 1M, Green Hornet microphone, Knight-Kit C-577 compressor-preamp and a Collinear II antenna. That is the setup I had the longest and that I have the best memories of operating. At different times I had a D104 (amplified and non-amplified,) a couple of Shure 444T's, a Green Hornet and various hand mikes. I had a Courier 1M, a LRE HE20D, a Knight Kit CB, various 525 & 625 radios, an HB-50 SSB mobile radio, HE-29B walkie-talkies, 5-watt 23-channel HT, and the LRE Telsat SSB-100 AM/SSB transceiver. My first outdoor antenna was a LRE quarter-wave ground plane. I never had a linear amplifier. I think I was too afraid of the FCC and losing my only way out.

Equipment came and went. I had little money and what money I had was being saved toward a car. That was my ultimate weapon of escape. My first car was a dark blue 1966 Corvair. I had a special love for that car. It was my first. I have never felt the same way about any car since. My first mobile radio was a LRE HB 525. I am not sure if it was a 525A, B or C.

The biggest item I ever bought new was the Knight-kit compressor preamp. I bought it as a kit and put it together myself. I still have that original unit I wired up and soldered.

Don (The Air Raider)

Don had a Courier Range gain CB and two of his special 1 transistor "wonder" preamps in series and a Green Hornet microphone. I think he had the two stacked three element beams before Dan did. He also had a Kris 200B linear amplifier.

Ted (Night Owl)

Ted had a Comstat 25A Long John 5-element beam, a Vibatrol preamp and green hornet microphone.

Barry

Barry had a Super magnum antenna, a Comstat 25A, and a Shure 444T microphone.

The Curiosity

The Curiosity had a LRE Comstat 23, Mark V. I had the unfortunate pleasure of trying to "tune-up" his radio while on its side and having it fall over on a piece of metal. The stars must have been aligned just right (or wrong depending on how you looked at it,) and the plate voltage connected with the series tube heater circuits. It is true what they say about burning bright and lasting only a short time. Well at least it was true with these tubes anyway! He left the radio with me to "fix" and borrowed another radio. It seems I can still hear him asking the same question (he always asked when he heard me on the radio.) "How's my Comstat?" Well, I'll finally tell ya, she was a shining star for oh too short but she didn't make it for the long run!

Joe Cannonball

All I know is he seemed too high on life (or something,) and had a bevy of young teenybopper beauties at his disposal. I was more interested in the latter than I was the former! I did get to give them a ride in my green Chevrolet Nova with Mark (Starship.)

9 - The Hazards associated with CB Radio

The Lure of the Sexy, diminutive voice

One of the hazards associated with CB radio was talking to girls on the radio then finally meeting them in person. Sexy little voices turned out to be economy-sized people! Not to be sexist, this was often the case for the guys as well, but that didn't matter to me as much! I guess it was one of the intrinsic, both hazards and benefits, of CB radio. You "saw" people as they portrayed themselves, not as they looked. You could either get to know the inner person or get a "larger than life" mental image from the voice. However, when the curtain was whisked away, you were often faced with a physical representation that didn't come close to matching the mental image you had created. I guess it might have been the same for the purveyor of the image. Their physical image did not match the mental image they held or wished for themselves. Two exceptions to the rule were "Island Girl" and "Hotbox Mobile!" They both met and exceeded all expectations of their voices and handles!

As I got to know people in the group, my image was much more outgoing and friendly than I was in person. It was the way I felt inside but I didn't show in person.

Ya better be good, Ya better not curse, cause Uncle Charlie is coming to Town!

You might have wondered where the FCC was in all this. There was a substantial gap between the FCC's intended use for the Citizens Band and the reality. It was supposed to be all call letters and no profanity. The legal limit was five watts maximum input and no black boxes (linear amplifiers) or preamps that caused extensive over modulation and interference. The FCC was code named "Uncle Charlie." Why that was, I don't know. When Uncle Charlie was in town, the word spread faster than an SBD (silent but deadly) fart in an elevator. Soon as one offender got written up, everyone was on their best behavior. If you weren't a major offender, you got off with a first warning. If it was a major offense like using high-power, illegal equipment or causing major interference, you were fined, had all your equipment confiscated and might have to make a court appearance. All this was bad enough but dealing with your parents was (by far) the worst part!

Don't Get Mad, Just get even!

Pinning the Coax – One of the ultimate ways of "getting even" with another CBer, and one of the hazards you might incur, was the pin in the coax. This was only used if all else failed. It was used when the relationship progressed from dislike to extreme hatred. I guess it was better than physical violence. Most of us used coax to connect our transceivers to the outside antenna. Coax has a center conductor, a concentric insulating layer then a braided shield and then another (usually black) insulating layer. To "Pin" somebody's coax, you would push a push-pin in with pliers far enough to touch both conductors but not far enough to break through the skin of the other side of the black outer insulator. Then you would cut off the rest of the pin and push it in slightly with another pin. The hole in the black insulator would seal after the pin was pushed in and an undetectable short was inserted on the antenna cable! This usually necessitated replacing of the entire coax as you couldn't find the short circuit. Even if you did find the short, you had to cut the cable at that point and would not have enough cable to reach the antenna anymore.

Jamming – Using one of the methods indicated such as "throwing" a dead carrier, sound effects, music voice clips or using funny or disguised voices to cause interference between two or more CBer's trying to have a conversation.

10 - School Daze

When Worlds Collide...

There was a drastic transmogrification from my radio persona to my high school image. It was not an intentional image. I identify a lot with the movie "My Bodyguard." If you saw this movie, I identified with the big kid in the army jacket (I had one just like it!) He supposedly killed his brother. The difference was that I had a huge amount of frustration and anger built up inside me instead of self-guilt. I was two halves of critical mass just waiting for someone to give them a nudge that would push them together. I never looked for a fight and I was always quiet. Nevertheless, there were a few incidents where others thought they could make points with the class and make themselves a bigger man by putting me down and making fun of me in gym class. I do remember lifting a kid off his feet, by the neck, with one hand. I backed him into the wall, griped his throat, pushed him up there, and held him there. I remember the gym teacher beating on me trying to make me release my grip. I think it was because of this or one or two other incidents that I received special permission to be excused from gym class. I was allowed to workout on the universal gym and go swimming if I wanted to. I don't remember asking for this arrangement. I think it was suggested by the gym teacher probably in response to one of the incidences in gym class. I don't remember much from that time. The weight machines were great for working off excess frustration. I had plenty to go around!

The Zombie Life

Life on the radio seemed more real than face-to-face interactions. My radio room was my "Fortress of Solitude." I locked myself within its soundproof walls and was then able to talk until any hour of the night or early morning hours without disturbing my parents. When we talked on the radio, we communicated what we felt at that moment. There was much frustration, mixed emotions and young male posturing. There was more truth in the midnight hours. We weren't in the "in-crowd." We weren't well dressed, or on the football team or outspoken at school. We were the invisibles, the ignored and the untouchables. I speak for myself about this. I only can guess what it was like for the other guys.

School life was a painful existence that had to be endured. Coming home to CB radio was the reward. Most of the kids who expressed themselves in school seemed like jerks to us. School life was like watching life in black and white. I went through school in a daze like a zombie. Every school day was one more day to make it through. My reward experiencing my real life on the radio. Talking on the radio was rich 3-D color! I hardly spoke in school and you could not shut me up on the radio!

We, as human beings, like to categorize people into little prefabricated cubbyholes. This is a truism in high school. Once you were "pigeonholed" as an invisible, it was near impossible to ascend to the heights of a "superstar." When you have a fixed student population, only so many can be superstars and each of the rest of the categories. It was like being graded on the infamous "bell-shaped-curve." Only so many could get "A's." Everyone is rated compared to others in your class. When everyone is in a fixed position, everyone knows where he or she stands. When someone has the audacity to try to pull themselves from the "dregs" to join the "Olympians," it is an affront to them. It also has the effect of lowering their status in comparison! The competition in high school is stiff. I am talking about the social status not grades, although grades may play a part in your social status. As such, those of higher status guard it jealously. They hate to share it and vie to make themselves higher, or all those around them lower in status (which is sometimes much easier!) They wish to be the undisputed champions. It is hard enough to undermine the known competition without bringing an unknown into the mix! A common enemy is one of the few things that united the "Elite."

Hey, I am lost in this world too! Do you know that way out?

I was very lost in my high school and in my teenage years. It was painful and traumatic time for me. No one can feel and know your pain as intimately as you can. No matter what anyone else has been through, you will always feel the pain you have personally experienced the hardest and have it color your character the most.

I hurt for those other lost souls and wish to shine a little light to help guide their paths. I hope they find their way. I can't but try to help others if they appear lost or in mental anguish. It is my hope that I can make a connection and strike a resonant chord that has been lying dormant in someone else's psyche.

It is not my intention to pour salt in the wound but to help pull the thorn and stop the festering so the healing process can begin. I found my own path out of the darkness. I wish others the best in their search in finding themselves, peace, happiness, and love.

I hope you are able to put your past behind you and find the gentle peace that comes with acceptance by others as well by yourself. I hope you find the happiness of full self-realization. Lastly, I hope that you find and cherish the love of your life and are loved and cherished back in the way all human beings deserve. I know that I have!

Dan... Don't do that Dan. Dan...

I met someone in my chemistry class that I talked to over the CB radio. Usually the two worlds remained independent and had little to do with one another. My memory is a little murky about how Dan and I got to talking. I think we both arrived at class early. Dan must have come over to me and started talking. I was wearing my green muscle T-shirt. It was my "binkey," my good luck charm, my "blankie" and my favorite article of clothing. Some people had a favorite pair of pants, hat, blouse, skirt etc. I had my muscle-tee. I felt like it should have had a giant "S" emblazed on the front. When I wore it, I was indestructible or at least that is how I felt. I felt extra muscular and undefeatable. It gave me artificial self-confidence. That is like artificial intelligence except more artificial! I wore it too much!

At this particular time, I was more frustrated than usual and needed to release a megawatt of excess emotional and sexual frustration energy. Sherri would be in this class. I had to rid myself of it before my eyes glimpsed her sensuous body and my brain was short-circuited! I picked up a ½-inch diameter stainless steel ring stand pole and put it behind my neck. Dan said, "Oh so you think you are so strong. I bet you $10.00 that you can't bend that!" I then grabbed each end and let the force explode in my arms and shoulders. It turned into an over bent horseshoe. I had to unbend it a bit so I had enough room to pull my head out. I disregarded the pain I felt in my spinal column and in my neck, where the bar had rested. I put the pain somewhere else while I bent the pole. I guess I made it look too easy. I then bent it back to a wavy approximate straightness. "Wait, that was too easy! If you could bend it, so can I!" With that, Dan defoliated another ring stand of its base and beaker holding rings and placed it behind his neck. He strained until the veins bulged out in his forehead and neck and his face turned crimson. He let out an explosive breath, panted and was getting ready to try for the fourth time as I started to make faces at him. My eyes widened and I was trying to warn him.

"Are you trying to scare me? What? Can't you see that I am trying to concentrate on this? What are you trying to tell me? Don't tell me, Mr. McDonald is standing right behind me, right?" He said jokingly. I could only mutely nod my head. The only good thing was that Dan had not able to put so much as a noticeable bend in the pole, so all he had to do was reassemble the ring stand of the pieces and all was forgotten. Hey, by the way Dan, if you are reading this, you never gave me that $10.00! I figure with inflation and compound interest over 35 years, you owe me $1999.95!

AIR RAID!

The Air Raider got under my skin several times until we had the predictable confrontation. The thing was, I didn't care. I was a total introvert at school and CB radio was my only tie to reality. I was prepared to get my ass kicked if necessary. We went to the same high school together but I had never met him. I was a big kid (5' 11" and 225 pounds, and most of it was muscle.) I liked to work out to release my anger, frustration, and sexual tension. Working-out was one of my few emotional outlets. The way Don talked, I figured him for about 6' 4 or 5-inches and over 260 lb. He just became so overbearing on the radio that when he arranged a meeting I jumped at it. He was ruining my only social outlet. I didn't back down as everyone else had, which I found out later was what he had come to expect. I had enough of his threats. I went to Mr. Hacker's (Our shop teacher and a ham radio operator) electrical shop class to have our meeting after class was over.

Don was in the backroom hunting through Mr. Hacker's "Junk-box" for more transistors to try in his one-transistor monster audio preamplifier. I was a bit nervous, but determined. I was trying to regain my head of steam to prevent my legs from becoming wobbly. Don was famous for testing his one-transistor creations over the airwaves. He had a D104 microphone and a loud toggle switch that he could flip to put his latest version of the one transistor marvel into action. He would ask everybody and anybody the famous question, "How do I sound now, one, two, three to (CLUNK!), NOW, ONE, TWO, THREE!" He did more testing on the air than talking! I wanted to face this bigmouth and at least get an understanding, if not respect. Most of the kids were gone. There was only a couple left cleaning and finishing their experiments.

"Hey, is Don..." I hesitated. I was going to say the Air Raider! I didn't realize until this moment that I didn't know his real last name!

"Do you mean Don Wilson? He is in the backroom working on a preamp"

Don Wilson! He must be the Air Raider! I smiled and chuckled. It was all I could do to stop from laughing when I realized how preposterous my thoughts would have sounded if I said them aloud! I sounded like somebody just figuring out that Spiderman was Peter Parker or Superman, Clark Kent! It was all too true! We all had our alter egos and secret identities on the radio. We only shared our secret identities with those we trusted! I was about to enter the secret lair and unmask the "Joker!"

I decided logically, that since I was the superhero, then he must be my arch nemesis. I guess I felt like Superman or at least Batman only without Robin!

I boldly pushed past the little kids cleaning up and headed toward the backroom. I was reviewing Don's tirades over the airwaves and managing to get myself worked up to a full head of steam. I walked into the storeroom with an ugly expression on my face and there he was on one of those metal high lab stools. He had wide shoulders but not as big as mine! "Don!" He turned around dropping the transistors and parts that were in his hand. His eyes widened and his mouth dropped open. He whispered, "Are you Bob?" My face must have showed surprise and then became nastier than before. "Well stand up and let's get this going." His face turned a purple-red and he became shy and nervous. He mumbled a couple of words about his transistors and wouldn't look me in the eye. Finally, I convinced him to get off the stool and he disappeared! He was short! He looked like one of the characters in a cartoon that got squashed by an anvil! Not only was he smaller than I was, he was a shrimp! A fight between us wouldn't even be a contest! I was looking for the "Joker" and got the "Penguin" instead! He was so nervous and scared and he became scarlet-faced, drenched with sweat and began to stutter. I began to feel sorry for him, especially after I beat the ever-living crap out of him! No, I didn't beat him up but I couldn't resist saying that I did! It helps release some of the inner tension I still feel.

Well, I never had a problem with Don after that. I guess after that "meeting of the minds" we arrived at a mutual understanding without ever having to discuss it. I read this and I feel I have been excessively harsh. Don was a good-looking guy but just short. I think he let his Napoleon complex rule his life so he had to appear that much larger than life. I also think it influenced him to show-off in front of us. If he had, only let down his guard a little and curbed his sticky fingers and dangerous car theatrics… Who knows, maybe we could have been friends.

Hello, I am the Invisible Man, and you are…

I remember another incident from high school. I was in a study hall area with circular wood tables, near the stairwell to the first floor. I was holding onto my books just watching and killing time. Two attractive, young women happened to meet and strike up a conversation in my immediate vicinity. For some reason or other, they decided to talk about me as if I wasn't there and evaluate my clothes, hair, and body musculature. Maybe they thought I was enraptured by their dazzling wit or I was staring at them.

I often stared out into space. I was looking at places, people, and things no one else could see. There were few times when I visited reality. I went through high school in a trance. Maybe I was too sensitive and maybe they were trying to talk to me, but I took it as an attempt to embarrass me and put me down in public. When they got to the "well he wouldn't be half bad if he could lose the coke bottles," I lost it. I had so much frustration and loneliness pent up inside me, I was a ruptured gas line in search of a match. Some imaginary switch flipped in my head and someone else took over my body. Some other facet of me took over the controls. I couldn't stop it or say a word. One of the scariest things was, I had no idea what my body was going to do next! I slammed my books down on the nearest table with a resounding gunshot sound. I then boldly strode over and then grabbed the closest girl and snatched her off her feet. There was no sensation or effort involved. I grabbed her into my arms, locked her startled eyes to mine, and bored into her soul. She seemed paralyzed and pliant. Her eyes went wide in surprise, shock, or fear and then got lost in the moment. I slowly dipped her over and kissed her on the lips, slowly, and passionately at first and then fiercely. Nobody was more surprised than I was at what my body was doing! I had been afraid I was going to hurt her! The thought never occurred to me that I would kiss her! Then all sound became muted and my focus became her. We were the only two people, which existed. I think I must have released all the pent up loneliness, passion, frustration, and hunger in that one kiss. I think for the first time, in those short moments, I felt loved. In these moments I was accepted at school. I had friends who knew the real me and liked me for my mind and soul. I had a girlfriend and we were in love. Passion was part of our relationship but it was the passion of being soul mates and knowing, accepting and cherishing our minds and bodies. I was a part of the human race and I was happy. Life was ecstasy! In those moments, I knew a happiness I never even admitted to myself that I yearned for. When I opened my eyes again, the spell was shattered and my soul turned to stone. I looked down and all I could see was another one of my tormentors. It was the catalyst, like a rock thrown into a lake that was well below freezing, which was all it needed to turn the lake as well as my heart to ice. I could feel the tears of frustration begin to well in my eyes. Her eyes were still closed and she had a dreamy look on her face. She had apparently gotten into the mood of the kiss. As fast as I had swept her off her feet, I dropped her like a broken, discarded doll. She crumpled to the floor lifelessly. I picked up my books and angrily trudged off without ever looking back. I didn't stick around to hear what was said, who they were or what the reactions were. I guess I will never know, unless these words reach one of you that were there! If so, please let me know! I often wonder what it was like to be on the other side of one of my crazed impulses! I did say I was a misfit didn't I? I never meant to hurt anybody except maybe myself. My mind was tormented back them but I assure you that I am normal now! I am being serious! Aaaw, come on! You believe me, right?

It's Alive! It's Alive!

I had much time to think in high school, sometimes too much. After high School, I began a task that young women learn early and are experts at when they are women. I started to critically evaluate my continence in the mirror. The overriding reaction was the coke bottles had to go. I made contacts a high priority on the list. A hairstyling was next. I had always dieted and worked out. Clothes were the next. Last was the installation of a software switch in my brain. I knew I could do it. It was "flipped" once before under a moment of high stress. Why couldn't I learn to use it to my advantage? I practiced and found the switch and refined its properties. When I flipped that switch, I was on the prowl. There was no sense of inferiority, being invisible or ignored. I only exuded self-confidence and sensuality. I was ultra-visible. I basked in it and fed off it. I acquired plenty of female companionship but not love. You can reinvent your looks, appearance and actions but not your heart. If you can't open it enough to make it available, nobody will be able to take it (or break it.)

Sex rears its Ugly Head

OK, you knew this was a book about coming-of-age. It had to come up eventually. Many might find this distasteful but here it is. If you might be offended by raw adolescent teenage sex, as seen through the eyes of a teenager during this time, please skip this section and move on to the next section.

There is nothing on a male teenager's mind more than sex, girls, kissing, sex, making-out, hugging, sex, petting, dancing, love, sex... Well you get the drift. It's a biological imperative. It's in our genes and we had to try hard to keep in our jeans! We looked at girls with unabated lust and wanted a girlfriend, a lover and a sex kitten. It's human nature and the rage of hormones that are out of control in the teenage years.

Most of us didn't have the verbal skills, the self-confidence or the social skills to interact with the fairer sex. So, we used CB radio to talk big and inflate our egos. This did change eventually, for most of us. Some of the young women we met on CB were a tad more advanced in experience and were aggressive. Take "Hotbox Mobile," I did. With a handle like that, you expected a hot, vivacious, sensuous woman. This is one of the few cases that your expectations were exceeded by astronomical amounts!

C'mon baby make it hurt so good! Sometimes love...

Another incident seared into my brain synapses, occurred in Mr. McDonald's chemistry class. He was an excellent teacher and a better human being. I had an intense crush on Sherri, one of the young women in class. My reaction to her didn't leave enough blood in my circulatory system to allow both "brains" to work correctly in class. She sat in front of me and I was enthralled by the scent of her body and perfume. Where was the scent emanating from? Where had she placed the perfume? These and other provocative thoughts kept me enticed.

The curve of her breasts and the musculature of her legs were my Kryptonite. I stared at her covertly awaiting a glimpse of her thighs, the swaying of her bountiful breasts and ample cleavage or a chill reflected in her erect nipples straining against the fabric of my existence. I never got the courage to talk to her. I did stupid things to draw her attention. It was the pigtails in the inkwell thing. I once put a container of Ban roll-on deodorant on her desk. It wasn't because she ever smelled anything but "oh so fine." It was just because I couldn't express what I felt and it was boiling over inside. She got flushed and proceeded to smack me with her hands. Her touch was like fire on my body. I didn't feel anything but pleasure from her hands. The more she hit me, the bigger I grinned. I think I could have gotten into S and M in a big way if this ritual had continued! I guess any reaction was much better than no reaction! It was much better than being treated like an invisible or non-person!

Unrequited Lust is like a water balloon...

I came to class early and was fooling around in the classroom picking things up and examining them. I found an eyedropper with a surgical rubber squeeze bulb. I had never seen surgical rubber used in this application before. It made me wonder how far it could expand and how much pressure it might exert. It brought my mind back to a toy I had much fun with as a kid. It was a water rocket. It consisted of two parts. The first part was a fat, green, transparent, 7-inch long, plastic rocket. (Before you go off "half-cocked", just remember, sometimes even a rocket is just a rocket (as long as it's not in your pocket,) even a 7-inch long one! The second part was a yellow and blue pump. Water not provided! You filled the rocket up with water and then applied the pump and pumped it up as many times as you could. You then aimed it for the stars (or one star, the sun) and pushed the red release button. The rocket shot off amid a gushing spray of water being ejected from the tail end. Yes, it was Freudian! The fun usually ended with the rocket on the roof or lost. My perpetual frown cracked and a smile momentarily crept across my face and lips. I loved that little rocket!

I looked over at the faucet. We were in a Chemistry Lab. They had big stainless steel sinks with a large chrome faucet that looked like a large, upside-down "J." The spout was concentrically graduated so you could push a rubber hose on it for science experiments. On a whim, I pushed the eyedropper bulb over the graduations onto the spout. I turned the long, flat, bat-handle of the cold-water facet on to produce a small trickle of water. I thought it would make a little pop as it shot off in class and I could take credit for it with Sherri and use it as an icebreaker. I went back to my desk feeling satisfied with my plan.

Today was the day! I was going to talk to Sherri today! I was determined! This was the end of sitting around and daydreaming! It was time for some action! I was all smiles and my nerve endings twitched and jangled with the electric feelings of anticipation and excitement! I would talk to her and she would see I wasn't really a "nut-case" like I appeared. We would date and then go to the drive-in and my hands would be free to roam the range of her beautiful hills and valleys and explore the heavenly-forested entrance to her cave of love…

"Mr. Zito?" I was shocked back to the hated reality. The class was full and I looked at the clock. I had lost at least 20 minutes! The class was almost half over!

"Mr. Zito, please stand up and provide us with the answer!" It was the horror of all horrors. Mr. McDonald had caught me daydreaming, walked down my isle, and asked me to stand up and answer a question on his lecture! Unfortunately, the object of my desires and daydreams caused my secondary brain and head to have the same intense reaction. I started stuttering, tried to rearrange my wooden friend, and stood up. There was a total unreality to the situation. It was like one of those dreams where you went to school and realized you had forgotten your pants. My mind was fragmented. Maybe it was because I was startled out of my daydream, maybe because I wanted it too badly. Random things went through my mind as it drifted. One of the things I wondered about was if the eyedropper ever did its thing. I glanced over at the faucet and I took a double take. There was a volleyball sized water balloon burgeoning and bouncing around, hanging from the spout! At that moment, Sherri turned around and was almost face to "face" with my uncomfortable bulge. It was embarrassing but exhilarating and undeniably sexy! She looked up at me and smiled seductively. She then started running her tongue over her lips. My eyes were drawn to her lips. Nothing else mattered. She made an "O" with her lips and stuck out her tongue. She then pantomimed licking a Popsicle.

"Mr. Zito!" That reality abruptly ceased to exist and I was relentlessly thrust into the old one. Mr. McDonald stood there facing me. "Mr. Zito, when I said that I wished my students would have a "love affair" with science, this was NOT what I meant!" He said as his eyes transfixed my bulge with the avenging sword of Damocles. The class broke into laughter and catcalls. My face began to feel sunburned and I could feel it pulsing in rhythm with my galloping heartbeat. I shifted my weight rapidly back and forth between each of my legs like I had to take a brutal whiz. I was uncomfortable and not able, at that particular moment, to adjust my now perpendicular appendage to a more reasonable position. It was locked and loaded. I was in the condition that males get that sometimes causes it to "lock-up" even after the initial emotions that caused its erection have long gone. There was some truth to it having a mind of its own! The worst part was Sherri looking at me with extreme revulsion and disgust, not admiration. It was spotlighted in her withering gaze. It was as if I were struck deaf and dumb. My mind was paralyzed. I just stood there unresponsive to Mr. McDonald's questions and my eyes kept being drawn back Sherri's exposed cleavage, Mr. McDonald and the now watermelon sized eyedropper bulb. Mr. McDonald, from his higher vantage, followed my gaze down to Sherri's blouse and generous cleavage and almost got lost there too. He must have had an excellent view of heaven! He abruptly cleared his throat, harrumphed, and got noticeably flustered.

Mr. McDonald then quickly whirled around and saw the eyedropper. "Oh you guys! I thought you would be out of the water-balloon phase by now! "No, don't do it," I yelled but, I just really thought it loud because I still couldn't talk. Have you ever been thinking intently about something and then yelled a warning to someone, but you never actually spoke? You finally realize that you only yelled it in your mind. Well this is how it was. At first, I thought I yelled but I hadn't. He strode right over and pulled the eyedropper off the graduated faucet. I have no way of calculating the forces, but that eyedropper could not be blown up like that from human lungs. The pressure must have been enormous. The bulb forcefully released all of its contents in a small fractional part of a second. The resulting "fire hose like" release blew away Mr. McDonald's glasses and sent his hairpiece scuttling across the room. He had been in the middle of opening his mouth to talk when this occurred. He looked like a drowning victim being pulled out of the violent surf. He was coughing and sputtering up water from his lungs through his mouth and nose. The class was transfixed. He finally cleared his throat, wiped his eyes, and blotted his face with the old handkerchief he always carried in his blue, lab-jacket pocket. He raised his hand with an accusing finger, ready to point the indictments and shook it like you would in chastising a child. He whirled around and faced us.

"Oh, you guys! Always with the jokes! Read chapters 7 and 9 in your chemistry texts and do all 10 sample problems at the end of each chapter for the next session and you, Mr. Zito, come prepared next time, without your little friend!" That was it! There were no other repercussions! Mr. McDonald was a sweetheart!

I didn't know at the time that he had inoperable cancer and that he was dying. I never did get the courage to talk to Sherri after that. She made it a point of coldly ignoring me and not acknowledging my presence at all. The transmogrification was now complete! I had become so monstrous, I became invisible to the person I had cared about the most. OK, well maybe the person I lusted for the most! I think it was another divining time in my life. If the situation had gone my way, maybe I could have made friends or even a girlfriend. Well I guess you have heard the old "coulda, woulda and shoulda" line before. Nevertheless, the truth is you (and I) will never know what could have been. Maybe there was no chance at all and I was just kidding myself. Well, life goes that way. You usually only second-guess the times you fail miserably at it. It didn't go my way this time and I just shrank back from this reality and found a better world. I gave up at trying my meager and sporadic attempts to fit in then.

As the guys started meeting girls and having girlfriends and experiencing the "Joy of Sex", priorities changed. Whether on CB or not, this was often the case. When a guy had a serious girlfriend, love affair, or "lucky streak," he usually was noticeably absent from the airwaves. Sex conquers all! There was no thought of social responsibility, disease, or possible outcomes. At most, a condom was revived from its secure crypt in the innermost recesses of your wallet. I was no better than the rest. Once I transformed myself and found I could be successful in the meeting, dating, and mating, I discarded CB like a snake does his old skin. In many ways, I regret that. You have to have friends. Life is just too lonely without them. Lifelong friends from your childhood are irreplaceable. They bring continuity to your life. They know you from the old days. No matter how much you would like to deny it, the present, social, butterfly (that you are now) was spawned by the ugly, awkward caterpillar. You can't deny it to someone who knew you back then. To say the past is irreverent to your present personality is again not possible. It is still contained inside you and is a part of your present personality. Some people evade their childhood friends so they can deny the existence of an awkward or painful youth. They think that if they eradicate all reminders from their youth, they can surgically expunge these things from their persona. The scars remain no matter how many layers of silk and polish you apply over the sow's ear.

I knew you couldn't resist reading this section! We can't. We are human and sex sells!

11 - I was a Teenage CB Werewolf and other growing pains

Working for a living – The Night Shift

I worked for the Security, Detective Agency when I was 18 years old. I became a rent-a-cop and worked at the Mid-Island shopping mall in Hicksville New York (Which was on Long Island) during the day shift. There was a guard there we nicknamed "Crazy Ernie." The management started noticing holes in the ceiling of the plaza and wondered what caused them. I had no clue. One night when my replacement called in sick, I pulled a double-shift at the mall and I met Ernie for the first time. The mall was all shut down and Ernie was showing me his "fast-draw" with his service revolver. As we walked past some bushes, we frightened some pigeons and they took flight. Ernie proceeded to quick draw and emptied six shots at them! So now, I finally knew where the holes in the ceiling had come from!

Another time, when I worked the late shift with Ernie, the plainclothes security people from one of the stores were making a bank drop (deposit) at the Malls internal bank. Ernie came up to me and was acting like a co-conspirator and whispered. "Wanna have some fun? Watch this!" He waited until the two nervous looking security people were at the crossroads (the place where each of the malls two branches met) and he took out his service revolver and opened fire on them. They dove for the garden beds, which was the only cover available. There were center flowerbeds down each of the mall branches. The garden beds were surrounded by a small, mortared rock wall. The rock was cut stone and had a jagged, sharp face. The security men whipped out their 38s and frantically looked for a target. Then Ernie yelled out in a theatrical voice. "What's the matter boys? Are you having a problem?" He then began to laugh in an over exaggerated manner.

"Son of a bitch, Ernie! One of these days you are gonna get a 38 slug right in your fucking fat head!"

"OK, OK Ralph, calm down, no harm done!" his partner said trying to calm him down.

"For Christ sake!"

"No harm done!"

"I'm fucking bleeding! That sounds like harm to me!" The sharp rock face had done its job. One man had cuts on his face and the other on his arm.

Ernie just chuckled and said, "Those boys love me! I keep them on their toes!"

I was in shock!

"Someone could have been hurt!"

"Naw," He said as he flipped open the cylinder of his gun and ejected the spent shells and started putting new bullets in the cylinder one at a time. "I replaced the real bullets with some blanks! I was just funning with them!"

Ernie's days at the Plaza were numbered. His time at the Plaza ended one day in the truck tunnel underneath it. The guards on the night watch, we were expected to make the rounds. We carried a round metal time clock in a black leather case with us. This clock marked the time and had a keyhole for inserting a clock key. At various places in the mall, a little box held a coded key on a beaded metal chain. You opened the box, took the key out, inserted in the clock and twisted clockwise. This put a code on the internal tape that showed the time you walked past that particular station. This was done to make sure the guards made the rounds and were prevented from sleeping or goofing off on-the-job.

A truck tunnel ran underneath the mall and gave truck delivery access to each of the stores. Ernie was making rounds one night when he spied a car in the middle of the truck tunnel. The cars lights were off and the engine was running. There were two kids in there with their clothing half off making out. Ernie comes down the steps to the roadway in front of the car at the far side and draws his revolver and yells, "Everyone out of the car, you are all under arrest!" Well the kid at the wheel panicked and floored the accelerator and Crazy Ernie (true to his name) stood there in front of the car "Dirty Harry style" and emptied his revolver into the rapidly approaching car. He did manage to dive for cover at the last instant with an "Oh, Shit!" No one was hurt, but when management found out, it was the end for "fast-draw" crazy Ernie.

After I worked as a guard there, they were finishing a new office building and a guard was needed. I was to work there as a guard until shortly after it was finished and open for business. This building was shaped in a concave, quarter-circle. All the windows were mirrored glass. It was an attractive building. It was a boring summer job and I longed for the other young people at the Mid-Island Plaza.

I was there during the first brutal days of the summer. It was 105 degrees out and close to 100% humidity. The building was air-conditioned so I was comfortable while I was inside. A woman came over to my station and wanted me to look at her car. There was something wrong with it but I couldn't quite understand what she was trying to tell me. I left the "oh so comfortable" air-conditioning and went into the unbelievable heat. It felt more like 128 degrees out there and the sun was reflecting off the building viciously. Her car had been in the full sun all-day and I burned my fingers by just touching it. I tried to look in but all the windows were darkly tinted. I still didn't see what the problem was or what she wanted me to do.

"Miss, I don't see what the problem is!"

I just wanted you here while I opened it as I didn't know what to expect with the windows and all."

I was mystified and I think I was getting sunburned already! I was sweating like a porker and I just wanted to get out of the sun and back into the gorgeous air-conditioning. I was out of patience and getting dizzy. It was unbelievably hot.

"Look, just open it, as I have to get out of this heat!"

"OK, OK!" She stuck her key in the lock and turned it. She touched the handle of her door, screamed, and let go. It was so hot it left a nasty red mark on her fingers.

I looked around for something I could wrap around my hand so I could open the door without burning my myself. I saw an old partly burned McDonald's bag and I bent over to grab it and almost passed out. I had to get back in the air-conditioning. I felt like I was on fire! I grabbed the handle and pulled open the door and the car compartment erupted into flame! We backed up and I woozily made it back to the building. The air-conditioning hit me like a cold wave of water. I looked in the mirrored walls and I looked sunburned! I called 911 and the fire department and they managed to get the fire out before the car exploded. I found out later the building's mirrored windows were set precisely! Most of them focused the sun on that one parking spot. The firefighters said that it was over 200 degrees in focus of those windows! It was much hotter inside of the car. We were both badly sunburned just standing there for the few minutes we were there! The fire department cooled down all the cars and the building was evacuated. They had glaziers reset all the windows so they never focused the light of more than one window on a parking space! I have never heard of this in the news at the time, or anything like it since!

Vegas with Aluminum blocks – what were they thinking?

When members of our group passed their driver's tests, it was time to buy a car. Chevrolet Vegas were popular models. They were sporty looking, not too slow, with a four-speed manual transmission, and cheap! They had one other hidden feature; the engine block was made from aluminum! While this made the car light, it also made the motor sensitive to stress.

Teenagers should be the stress expert's car manufacturers hire to discover if their car could "cut-it" in the real world. Dan and Mark both purchased one of these beauties, as did my father. They looked especially good in red. The guys used them in drag races, road rallies and in general, hard use. I think the guts of this car was designed for grandma to use to and from church on Sundays and the outside was made to look like a sport car.

They sold many of them before the engines started having "meltdowns."

You can Talk to the World

Once I was married for the first time, I turned back inward for solace. I yearned for my friends again. Not only had the group broken up, CB radio was no longer the same nor would it ever be. At my first job, I met Al. He was the strange mad-scientist type and he was also a licensed Amateur Radio operator, colloquially know as ham radio. He was my "Homer," the mentor which helped me get my amateur radio license. He encouraged me to get my "ticket." I got the books and the code tapes and decided that this time I was going to do it! I had no more excuses or needs for a ride to the testing locations. I got my novice license and bought a Viking ranger II from Al. It was a high-power CW transmitter. Pound for pound, it was a great deal. I had a Hallicrafter's HQ110C for a receiver. I sent and received Morse code for just under a year and then decided to upgrade.

I went from Novice to Advanced in one-shot. I had fun and enjoyed it but it still wasn't the same. I think I was subconsciously looking to bring back the old times and friendships. Of all the guys from the old CB radio days, Mark was the only one still around and still interested.

I upgraded my low-band equipment to a Kenwood TS-520 (with analog dial. Digital was yet to come!) One of my first unintentional contacts with this radio was the FCC monitoring station in Texas. They were kind enough to send me a confirmation ticket asking me to explain why I was 96 Hz lower than the allowed frequency! I sent a letter apologizing profusely and I bought a frequency (B &K model 1801) counter. I used it for all frequency calibrations after that! Next, I upgraded my Clegg FM-27A 2-meter radio to the newest, hottest radio on the market. The FM-27A radio was a synthesized radio with several potentiometers. You adjusted them to point to the right number silk-screened on the front panel. You always approximated the frequency you were on and had to "fine tune" the controls for maximum signal to match someone else's frequency. If you happened to brush against the dials, you could be happily broadcasting anywhere in the two-meter band!

My replacement 2-meter radio was a synthesized radio that covered the entire 144-148 MHZ band and had an orange-red digital LED display. It also had high-power! It was the Clegg FM-28 with the highest power available in a mobile radio! It had 25-watts of power and no memories! I think I paid $599.99 for this little beauty! OUCH!

I invited Mark over to the house to check out the nifty Amateur Radio equipment that I had. I tried to convince him to go for his ticket. However, he was hard to convince. I think he thought it too technical for him and the code would be impossible.

After what seemed like an eternity, Mark did get his Amateur Radio "ticket." The good old days came back for a while after that.

EEEK, the GEEK!

It was 1974 and I had a brand spanking new "piss green" Nova that I bought new off the lot for a ridiculously expensive price of $3500.00. The car had an 8-cylinder 350 cubic inch engine and I wanted to put a CB in it. It was my first new car. My parents went to the lot with me as they were co-signing my loan. They wanted to be home and in bed. They gave me a choice of buying this car on the spot or not co-signing the loan. The car had the right engine but I hated the color. It ended on growing on me like a cancer. The longer I had it, the more it ate at me, the more I hated it!

I was out in front of the house I was renting in Hicksville working on a CB installation on my Nova. I was working under the truck lid when I heard a voice. "Hey, what ya up to under there!" I looked up to see a small beat-up and rusted LeCar with peeling blue paint. The door opened and a tall, thin, mangy looking guy with red-rimmed eyes got out. He was wearing an old ripped army coat, torn dungarees coated with grease and a blue skullcap. He looked like a combination of a scarecrow, Maynard G. Kreebs, a bowery bum and Shaggy from Scooby Doo! He sounded like Mr. Haney from the Green Acres TV show. His hair stuck out from under the cap in a manner that just screamed, "I haven't had a professional haircut since the 60's." He hadn't shaved in a couple of days and his face was covered by gray-white stubble punctuated by a butt hanging out of the side of his mouth. All that was needed to complete the picture was a brown paper bag, hiding a bottle of Ripple, and a canting walk. For some "strange" reason someone called him "the Geek" and it stuck as his nickname. He spoke in a cigarette destroyed, hoarse voice. "What ya doing, installing a CB in your car?" I became instantly suspicious. Was this character trying to find out what I had so he could rip me off? "Ahhh...no. I am adjusting the SWR of my mobile rig."

"What kinda rig ya got?"

"It's a LRE Radio HB-625."

"Hey! What channel do you hangout on? Maybe sometime I can talk to you!" That would be about the last thing I would like to do!

"Well most of the time, I am on channel-10. What are your call letters?" I inquired.

"Oh, I'm using my brother-in-law's calls until I get mine!" he replied.

One day I was outside checking the SWR on my mobile radio again when the rusted out Le Car pulled up behind my car.

"Hey! I got something for you!"

I spoke under my breath, "I can hardly wait!"

He proceeded to the trunk of his car and pulled out a boxy shaped object covered by some dirty towels. "You are gonna love this!" He said in his cigarette burned voice.

"Wait till ta hear dis bomb! It'll knock yur socks off!" The "bomb" he was referring to was in a 10-inch square gray metal project box. It had a couple of switches, a plate, and tuning dial and a meter on the front panel.

"So what exactly is that supposed to be?" I asked.

"This here is the answer to your dreams!" It looked more like a nightmare to me!

"It's a home brew 200-watt linear and I can let you have it for only a hundred and a half! We took it in the house and I connected it up. I turned it on and it started humming. When I went to move it over a little, I saw it had a bunch of capacitors mounted on the back covered with insulation, which was then covered by aluminum foil. I assumed the foil was grounded and was used to avoid radio interference and provided a safety shield. I reached around the back and "ZZZZZAP!" I felt like I was being electrocuted! He was right about one thing. It did knock my socks off! I was touching and vibrating to plate voltage!

"Oh, I forgot to warn ya, you shouldn't oughta touch that! He cackled. "It can give you a real good zap!" he chuckled.

"Son of a bitch!" I yelled after I wrenched my hand away and stuck my fingers in my mouth.

"Whose bright idea was this? Did you build this kludge?"

"Nope! I just happened across it and I knew you would just love it!" I keyed up channel 10 and gave Mark a call. He came back after a few seconds. "Hey Starship are you on frequency?"

"Hey Survivor, what's happening?"

"I want to check something out. What is my signal reading now?"

"You are 20db over S9."

"OK, how about now?" I said as I threw the switch to put the amp on line.

"Just about the same except for a horrendous hum!" I turned around and looked at the Geek.

"Wow, that's some 200-watt amplifier!" I said.

"No, No, it must be his equipment! It works good and I am willing to give it to you for $100.00 cash!"

I put the amp on a metered dummy load and calibrated it for the 4-watt output of the Courier 1M. I then switched on the amp and just barely read 10-watts! After intensive tuning of the amp, I was able to get 12-watts and a huge 60-Hz hum out of it! Once again, I turned to the Geek.

"Tell you what, since you're my friend, I'll take $75.00 for this bomb!" The Geek said.

"Tell you what, since you are my friend, I will give you a 10-second head start then I am gonna beat the hell otta ya with this piece of shit!" He turned white. "You are only kiddin aren't…"

"Ten… Nine…Eight…" I started the countdown.

The Geek grabbed his amp and got zapped from that aluminum foil. "Ahhhhh!" He screamed.

"Sorry about that! I meant to warn you!" I said and smiled wolfishly. He disconnected the amp and took off out the door not to be seen for another couple of weeks.

The next time I saw that rusty color LeCar, with a just a dab of blue left on it, I was glad to see him! I had received my Amateur Radio license and wanted to put up a directional antenna. I used both amateur radio and CB band for a short while until Mark got his ticket too. I was going to put up an amateur radio "Mini Products" beam on top of my garage peak. I had the five-foot tripod already mounted to the roof. I had 10-feet of pluming pipe which connected to a Ham-M rotor and then five additional feet of pipe. The small, end-loaded, Mini Products beam was mounted at the end. I could use some help getting it in the tripod, especially since there were live power lines behind my house. The antenna was long enough to land on them if it were to fall.

"Hey you want some help putting up that bomb?" It was the only time I remember being glad to see him! He usually was a harbinger of doom! However, this time he could truly help me! He climbed up the ladder and I picked up the antenna that was wobbly because it was top-heavy. I had to try to balance it and walk up the ladder. The Geek grabbed a hold of the top portion of it to help me steady it. I walked it up the ladder and we were both on the roof. I was 5"11 and the Geek was maybe 6 foot. I probably had 100 lbs or more on him. When we tried to lift it up the 5-feet (we had to get it into the tripod,) the wind picked up and the antenna swayed toward the high-voltage lines. "It's gonna go!" Yelled the Geek as he let go of the antenna and jumped off the roof. I lowered the base of the mast back down to the roof and up against the base of the tripod and strained most of the muscles in my back and chest to bring it back to vertical.

"Get the fuck back up here and help me with this you asshole!"

"Huh, I thought it was gonna hit those high-tension lines!"

"Get up here now! This fucker is heavy!" We tried it one more time and managed this time to get it into the tripod. Once the antenna was in the tripod, I guyed down where it stayed for many years, until I moved to New Jersey. I hurt all over for the next couple of weeks but the Geek said that he hardly felt sore at all! I can't imagine why!

Can You Keep a Secret?

I was further down the time line of wedded isolation when Mark was down in the dumps too. I was driving my 1974, 350cc "Piss-green" Nova then. Almost any other color would have been better. This car had the engine and the features I had wanted but not the color. Well anyway, I was talking to Mark on the CB radio and he was down in the "dumps." I decided it was my turn to pick up his spirits. I got in the car and kept up the conversation. I got to talking to two young women that came on the frequency who were more bored than we were. I went over to their house and picked them up. I then asked Mark if he wanted to come along for the ride. I stopped by his house and got him. These young women were "hot to trot" and I was human but married. I started out doing a favor for a friend and began thinking about things. I was driving and screwing around trying to make Mark laugh. I was not happy with marriage now and I was going out with a group of people from work. One of the members of the group was a beautiful young blonde. I enjoyed talking to her. She was an intelligent woman, but she was broken and twisted inside. It was an irresistible combination. I went out with the group but it was mostly to be with her. We talked as close friends but I wanted more. My marriage weighed heavily on me now. I wanted to pursue her but I couldn't. She started dating a guy who was twisted in a hateful, controlling manner. It was a destructive relationship. All I needed to do was separate from my wife and I could pull her away from this creep. He introduced her to cocaine and I saw her slip away and become encrusted in a shell none of her friends could penetrate. She was teetering on the brink and he helped her make the big fall. I introduced her to Mark one night when he came down to a club we were at. He called her the "Ice Queen." He saw her as beautiful but, cold and dangerous. Once I "lost" her, it helped me make up my mind. It was time for me to make some big changes. I felt I had lost a chance at the one woman I could have loved. It angered me, frustrated me, and it decided me. In retrospect, I liked some of the ways her mind worked, but I don't think we would have made a go at anything more than friends.

My marriage had been over for a while in deed. It was time for legal action. I put it off because of guilt but end was drawing near and was precipitated by other things. This is the frame of mind I was in while we were driving around. I came close to breaking my vows. I came close enough to repeatedly ask Mark, "Can you keep a secret?" Something held me back. I couldn't do it. It was against what I believed in. I held truth and honesty in high regard. How could I break the principles that I held so dear? I dropped off the disappointed young women at their home, we drove around, and I tried my male bonding bit with Mark. We talked about important stuff like life, women and sex.

My worst trait, which I haven't been able to deal with too successfully, is the absence of good friend maintenance. I guess it is something that comes natural to most people. For me it is a chore. There are some unwritten rules that I am always breaking which get me into trouble. For example, there is a rule that if the other person called you last, it is your obligation to call next. Who came up with these rules and where can I get a copy? Mark is the one person who I have managed to stay in contact with for most of my life. It must have been because of great effort on his part. I know, from my history, that when I become focused on something, I forget about almost everything else.

The Power of the Red Balloon

Phil was a friend of Marks. He was more than a tad overweight and he had "gotten in good" with a relative of someone in the management of LRE. He could get anything from the catalog at "five-fingered" discount prices and sell them for half-price, or so the story went. He was always trying to sell us discount CB radios, scanners, amateur radios, and stereo equipment. Phil joined the volunteer fire department to be "one of the guys."

I (being the storyteller even at an early age) had created a graphic story involving high school pranks, getting even, locker-room disgusting stuff, and a red balloon. I told it to Mark as the truth. Mark was working part-time at a gas station and I came over to keep him company and pump some gas. We were there inside at a quiet time of the night. Mark kept on pestering me to tell Phil the story and Phil kept on denouncing the ability of anyone to make him sick. After all, he was a volunteer firefighter! He had heard, seen, and felt it all! He was a man of the world! He heard the grossest of the gross and his cast-iron stomach was bulletproof against the slings and arrows of anybody's morbid experiences.

It was a magic night and the story took hold of me and became reality in my mind. I recounted it like I never told it before. From a short five-minute treatise, I embellished in into a 45-minute novel. I saw the story take shape in my brain and breathed life into it. I began to see it in my mind like a situation that occurred. I lived it. I described the characters, their motivations, and their desires. I used two of the strongest of the black emotions that everybody can identify with, jealousy and revenge. I described the setup and the months of planning and preparation, that took place before the final high school football game. Then I described in excruciating detail the tactile, visual, olfactory and taste sensations. Mark started heaving and had to leave for fresh air. Phil was holding his wildly shaking, abundant belly with one hand and held the other over his mouth. As he fell down into a chair, hand over mouth, face all puffed out and scarlet he stammered, "Enough! Stop it! You're killing me! Enough!" Then he started to dry heave. This was my cue to go on with gusto! It was like a standing ovation to the stage performer! It is the highest compliment that an artist could seek! This was a feeling I had never felt before and I couldn't stop myself. I was out of control. I went into the minutest of details. The visual imagery with the recounted odors did him in. Phil fell from his chair to his knees. He was retching in earnest when Mark returned. The oily spots on the floor were covered with that garage floor stuff that absorbs oil spills and looks like kitty litter. Phil was on all fours retching, gulping, and blowing huge amounts of air that had the "kitty litter" blowing in waves. It looked like he had, and still was, blowing his cookies all over the place. He was dry heaving and viscous gouts of mucous-like fluids were dripping from his nose and mouth. The sounds combined with the "kitty litter" moving in waves made an incredible sight. Mark took one look, an amazed double-take and then a look of disbelief came over his face. Mark was laughing, heaving and tears were streaming down his face. It was followed by a white pasty look of wretchedness as he did an abrupt u-turn and scooted back out the door as his heaves returned in a big way. It was weird, Mark and Phil were laughing, crying, heaving and could be in imminent need of medical assistance. As Phil brought up what little contents and bile that remained in his stomach, he tried to do a push up from the floor and couldn't make it. He collapsed back into a mixture of his former stomach contents and the "kitty litter." His face was extremely swollen, red and blotchy and coated with a mixture of the litter, bile and mucus. He was gasping for breath, choking and pleading. He wasn't laughing at all this time.

"You're killing me, I'm dying, Stop it, oh God please stop it!"

I saw a picture in my mind of ambulances, police interviewers and the newspaper headline, "Fire-fighter is mercilessly talked to death." I stopped, Mark took that moment to return, and the reek of bile was overpowering. He was trying to talk, but he was laughing the painful laugh of the hysterical. Tears were fleeing from his eyes in sheets and he was holding his stomach. His face was an expression of pain. He took one look at Phil who looking like a giant, breaded, KFC drumstick from rolling in his own digestive juices and the floor litter. Then the overpowering smell hit him. He bolted back for the door. The only thing that had given me immunity was that I had been engrossed in the recounting of the story. Once the story was finally over, the spell was broken. I became one of the afflicted. I began retching and needed fresh air badly. I followed Mark out the door at a run and sat down on the curb. Slowly the fresh air took hold and the retching subsided. Both Mark and I looked up at the same time and locked eyes. We simultaneously burst out laughing and fell to the ground. We couldn't stop laughing. Our stomachs hurt and then become knotted, but we couldn't stop. It went on forever! We howled with both pain and laughter as our stomach muscles cramped and began to go into "charley horse" type knots. Every time it slowed down and was ready to dissipate, we would look up at each other and it would start all over again. We were sitting opposite each other supported by walls. We began trying to make each other laugh harder. We would gasp out short parts of comments between huge gulps of air and insane laughter. We volleyed back and forth "Phil...puke...guts...face...hands...ground...rolling...breaded...drumstick ...red...smell...belly..." Until we were out of breath and couldn't take it anymore. Finally, we closed our eyes and concentrated on gasping for air. We must have made some sight. We both collapsed on the ground, holding our stomachs, faces flushed and blotchy, incoherent, tears soaking our faces and clothes and pain creasing our faces.

I vaguely remember hearing the voices in the crowd at first indicating we looked like we had been shot to the assertions there had been a robbery and we had been stabbed and shot multiple times. There was even a description of the getaway car. I would hate to have one of these people be a "witness" to a crime I was being tried for! I was too exhausted and painfully sore to care. It hurt to breathe. I gasped for air. Both my ribs and stomach were extremely sore and it hurt just to breathe normally. I clearly heard the sound of sirens but it didn't register.

"Clear a path there! OK, break it up, the shows over!" I heard in the typical cop command voice. Someone leaned over us. "OK, buddy, where are you hit?"

Our eyes sprang open simultaneously and we took one look at the cop and each other and started laughing all over again. Only this time it was pure agony and all I could hear was a desperate, painful, wheezing-gasping sound. The searing pain was causing light to explode in my brain.

"Shit! I think they've been hit in the lungs! Get an ambulance! Is there anybody else in there? Where did the perpetrators go?" The questions were too rapid-fire for my mind. I focused on the first one and replayed it in my mind. Is there anybody else in there? Phil! Where was Phil? I tried to gasp out a message as it hurt to inhale, "In...side...he...still...inside"

"Tom! The "purps" are still inside! Call for back-up and break out the riot gun!" I tried to let him know he was my friend but it was too late. They weren't listening anymore. Everything took on a different cast, a nightmarish quality. The noises blended into the background noise. I was waiting for something. What was it? I was startled when

I realized that I had been waiting for the quasi-silence to be split with the crack of gunfire. Then it startled me when it came. Only it wasn't gunfire that broke and erupted from the silence, It was the high-pitched peals of surprised laughter. It seems the cops were also volunteer firefighters and they knew Phil. They had been trying to get back at Phil for the gross stories he told for months but couldn't pierce his "Cast-Iron" reputation.

They had found him in the garage, wallowing around on the floor "tarred and feathered" in his own excrement. They thought he looked like a breaded Pterodactyl drumstick! He was sufficiently recovered to recount the story amid peals of hysterical laughter. It looked like we were going to be here for a while.

12 - The Change of Life

Life, places, things, and times change no matter how much we sometimes don't want them to. Life has an inexorable way of trudging on like a faucet dripping slowly into a sink with a closed drain. Each individual drip of water adds an imperceptible additional amount of water but the next morning the sink is full to the brim. Where these past 42 years have gone is a mystery to me. I write this and can't believe they are gone. There is little left except the memories and someone to share them with.

We weren't the original pioneers of CB radio. We weren't even the first in our area. We were the first group of kids in our area to take control of channel-10 and make it our home. We saw channel nine become reserved for "React" and thought it was a good thing. Then the truckers found out about CB radio and channel-19 became trucker's heaven. That whole business of talking with a southern accent and creating the entire CB lingo rankled me. This was not what CB radio was to me. I am sure that for some, who came in at this time, this was proper and felt right. That wasn't where I came in. It was a much warmer, friendlier, hometown place for me. It also was my way out of exile. It was a close friend and confidant. To me, it began to turn into a circus and the clowns were not funny.

Depending on the Sunspot cycle, the "skip" would come in and you would get people dedicated to chasing it. As more and more of the general populace "discovered" CB, I found that it lost its unique charm. In addition, we grew up, matriculated into society, and had girlfriends, lovers, wives and children of our own.

I matriculated to amateur radio to get away from the circus. I helped Starship make the transition too. We lived only a couple of miles away. We both bought Cushcraft 11-element Yagi beams and "locked" them on to each other. There was new radio out then. It was the Kenwood TR-7950. It was ahead of its time. It had an LCD backlit display, computer control and 50-watts output power.

There was a used TR-7950 advertised on a local swap-net. I took the information and Mark and I took a ride out to Centerreach (Eastern Long Island) to check it out. It turned out there were two friends each selling one. Mark bought one and I was undecided, as I couldn't get it for the price I wanted. One of the most enjoyable things I liked about buying used equipment was haggling for the price. I hated spending the money but if I could get it for a great price, I could feel it was justified. The second guy also had a maroon, 2-meter, Mirage SWR and Wattmeter up for sale. I wanted both and I wanted them for my price. A couple of days later we went back and I haggled until the second guy gave up and I picked up the other TR-7950 and the Mirage meter at my price. These radios had a low, medium and high-power settings.

We picked a frequency that was quiet and it became our new "channel-10." For a while, we reclaimed the old days. We lived about five miles away. We both had Hygain, 11-element, 2-meter, Yagi antennas. I modified our Kenwood TS-7950 radios for super-low power (100 milli-watts.) We were able to "lock beams," by pointing our antennas at each other and still get a strong signal with low power. This (in effect) gave us our own private channel. I was married at the time but not happy. Mark was single and dating with no significant other. We even purchased a repeater between us. The radios were always on and a friend was just a depress of the microphone button away. This was FM, so there wasn't any static, but there still was a squelch tail. When we talked on the radio, the changes and years melted away and we were temporally transported back to a simpler time. Talking to each other on the radio evaporated the stress of the daily grind. We both knew that we were living on borrowed time and cherished the time. I married, had a son, divorced and the financial burdens caused me to seek employment in other places.

After my separation from my first wife, I needed to get another job to be able to pay for all the bills I got stuck with. In Engineering you have to go where the money leads you. I took a job in New Jersey and commuted for 3-1/2 years. That finally became too much and I moved there. We didn't have communications in that arrangement. I commuted from Hicksville, New York to Paramus, New Jersey for 3-1/2 years. That is not what I intended to do. I figured that I could commute for 1-year while I decided if I wanted to keep the job. Then I gained a girlfriend in Levittown New York and it became harder to make that decision to leave. I kept putting it off. The trip in the morning wasn't that bad and I would talk to Mark every day on the way home by making use of various amateur radio repeaters. Although the distance was only about 50 miles, the traffic made the commute home a 2-1/2 to 7-1/2 hour nightmare depending on the weather, accidents, and road conditions. It was great to be able to spend that time talking on the radio. It made the trip almost bearable! I was adamant about keeping my cool and not letting the traffic snarls, the aggressive, idiotic drivers and the bad road conditions get to me. After all, I was talking with Mark and doing what I would be doing if I were home! If it didn't affect my spirit or my health then I could do it!

The end came when I was on line in the backup of traffic waiting to approach the George Washington Bridge. It was summer, 105 degrees with almost as much humidity. I was driving a big old Pontiac and it was overheating. I couldn't use the air-conditioning and I had to keep it in neutral and rev the engine to keep it cool. This caused me to wait until the car in front of me had edged up by a car length and a half before I would drop it in drive and catch up to it. I was swimming in a pool of my own sweat and I had a migraine headache coming on. I was determined to keep a cool head. Well the weather and the traffic had also been conspiring against the guy behind me. He showed his disagreement with my policy of letting the front car get a lead by "tap-dancing" on his horn. When that didn't get the reaction he wanted he started leaning on it. I put up my hands, shrugged my shoulders, and shook my head from side to side to indicate to him that I couldn't do anything about it. This enraged him. He revved his engine and rammed his car into the back of mine. He then reversed it, like a jumper wanting to get a good head start, and gunned it again. Each successive time he created a more severe impact. I was beginning to get a whiplash and doing a slow burn. I finally ignited on the 5th hit. I got out of the car ready to pull the weasel out of his protective shell and beat him to a pulp. He took one look at me advancing on him, with the look of death on my face, and rolled up all of his windows. I first kicked in both of his headlights and cursed him out like a raving lunatic. Then I ripped off his car antenna and proceeded to beat and scratch his car with it. I spidered his windshield and the drivers side window with cracks before I drained enough anger to regain my composure. I remember thinking that "This is nuts! I gotta stop this commute before something bad happens!" It was time to move! The old days were over. I couldn't reach Mark, on the radio, from New Jersey and life has a way of filling in the extra time.

I used to attend all the major Ham fests and "on-the-air" swap meets. Then his guy named Pierre came along with an idea of creating an "online" auction site. He was a hard worker and was always "fine-tuning" the user interface on his web site. He constantly asked for feedback on his little website. I felt sorry for the guy and was constantly giving him ideas on how he could improve the user interface. I was also selling my used equipment there without being charged a fee. Then one day, about a year or so after his creation spawned many users, Pierre created a poll questionnaire. He wanted to know how many people would still use his little service if he collected a modest charge, only if the equipment you listed was sold. The rest is history, the small website got larger and "EBAY®" was born!

13 - Whatever happened to the "Boys" of Channel 10?

Dan is married and has three "kids." He became a salesman selling major appliances in a local Sears store. A couple of years ago he moved to Georgia where he is a computer illiterate and hardly ever answers his e-mail. It seems as if he can't be bothered learning all that computer stuff. Mark ferreted out his telephone number from the Internet and had a two-hour mini reunion on the phone about 15-years ago. Their contact has been sporadic since then.

Barry showed us all up and became famous in his own right! We saw his picture in a New York newspaper and on TV at one of the States most prestigious Universities! Unfortunately, it was in the school's bell tower and he had a high-powered scoped, rifle! He was taking revenge for all the indignities and putdowns the world and society put him through. I am only kidding! I just imagined that happening and I am glad that it didn't! Barry moved to Arkansas to take over the family stereo business and finally got his Corvette. Actually, he bought seven of them so he could drive a different color and type each day of the week! Way to go Barry!

Don went to college and got his BSEE and his amateur radio license. We used to hear him every so often on the local repeater in the area. There was talk of things disappearing at work and he was let go. He had a hard time getting another job after that and was on unemployment. A couple of years ago, I heard that he opened a successful business called the "Lafayette Security and Detective Agency." It makes me wonder why he picked that name and who his clients are!

Ted still lives at home with his mother. He is no longer the skinny small kid he once was. I met him again about 20-years ago at a computer hobbyist meeting. He recognized me but I had no clue who he was. "Bob, Bob Zito?" He said in looking at me in surprise.

I turned around and regarded him without a flicker of recognition. "Ah, do I know you?"

"It's Ted!" He said as if I was supposed to know him.

"Ah, Ted…"

"Ted the Night Owl!"

"Ted?" It was my turn to stare. He was about three times the size of the thin, little kid I remembered. It's funny how we slowly change so we never notice a big change in ourselves but we expect people we knew from the past to still look the same as they did when we last saw them. Ted is now a computer enthusiast. He also works with and in, the computer industry.

Todd has a successful dental practice. Mark happened to bump into him one day and was too stunned to speak. The moment was over before he could say "Carpus Diem" and he followed him back to his office. There was a brass plaque outside his office that indicated Todd's name and DDS. When I found this out, it somehow reminded me of the Nazi dentist from "The Running Man."
I can hear him talking to the poor sod strapped down in the dentist chair.
"Is it safe?"
"What do you mean by that?" Asks a poor puzzled innocent Dustin Hoffman type character.
Then I hear the high-pitched whine of a dentist's drill slowing in pitch as it starts boring through tooth and bone as well as the screams of agony as Todd continues to drill holes through his "patients" front teeth and gums.

Phil moved to Florida and didn't keep in contact. Mark got a hold of his number and called him. They had a nice enough chat and Phil promised to keep in touch with Mark. Entropy has its way and voices from that past tend to try to stay there. He has never called back.

I was paging through an adult magazine about 22 years ago when a nude picture of two lovely ladies, with those "all over" tans, caught my eye. The article was entitled "Nudists in Florida." The young beauties were on either side of a huge bellied man with the same tan. Something about his huge belly and his nose struck a familiar chord and made me do a double-take. I braved another look at the rotund belly and the shrunken male equipment that heroically tried to prevent itself from being crushed by the overhang of flesh above it.

It was Phil! He was wearing the same oversize diving watch, black-framed glasses, and floppy fishing hat. I couldn't believe it! I called Mark and told him that he had to come over immediately. I had something to show him. He came over and I started showing him some of the beautiful women in the magazine. "You got me out of my easy chair for this!" He started to make like he was leaving. I casually turned the page to the small photo I wanted him to see.

"Look at the all-over tan on these babes!"

Mark glanced down at them. "Yeah, they look great but I gotta go. I became a little desperate.

"Wait, does anyone of them look, familiar?" I said with an edge in my voice. That caught Mark's attention and he picked up the magazine, scrutinized each of the women closely, and ignored the guy in the middle. He tossed the magazine back on the table.

"No, who do you think they look like, Island Girl or Hotbox Mobile?"

Then I sprung the trap and casually said, "Who said anything about the women?" Mark had a puzzled look on his face, glanced back at the magazine, and turned back to me to say something and it clicked. He did a double-take so fast that I thought would break his neck.

"What the fuck?" He grabbed the magazine back, and held it under the lamp. A look of pure amazement took over his face, he turned to me, and we both shouted "Phil," in unison. We started laughing. The years melted away, we were back in the same gas station once again. Phil was rolling on the floor breading himself like a huge brontosaurus drumstick all over again. We laughed and cried, our guts cramped, and we had to pause to catch our breaths. All it took was one look or one word to each other and we burst out in uncontrollable peals of painful laughter again.

I still talk to Mark mostly every day and we send many e-mails back and forth. We are both collector's of the LRE CB radios and catalogs. We also collect some of the amateur radio equipment we used in the "old" days.

H-Base - Moved with his family to Florida. Every 11-years or so, when the sunspot cycle peaks (the "skip" comes in) and the fog obscures the moors, there have been strange reports on channel-10. Witnesses say they have heard a mysterious, high-pitched, stuttering voice say "This KQD6140, H-base, Coco, Starship or AstroCookie can you hear me?"

Hotbox Mobile, Island Girl, H-Base, AstroCookie, Night Owl and Starship. These are all "handles" of people whose ghostly voices still call out to me. "How about it Survivor, are you still there?" I can still hear the voices in my head. I can still conjure up the faces of the kids we once were. They are voices from the distant past when I was growing up and learning to cope with and communicate in this sometimes cruel world. A world which isn't very friendly to the introverted, the different, the outcasts and the misfits. I reminisce about those days with a bittersweet feeling of loss, longing, and discomfort. I cringe at some of the things I did or didn't try to stop and sadness that I didn' take more joy in the days of my youth and the friends that were always there at the push of a microphone button

When life gets too stressful and I am in my darkened room either writing or surfing the web, I sometimes get nostalgic and think back to the days of old.

I will always have warm memories of the days of my youth and the quick companionship of the voice of a friend punctuated by static and a squelch tail. I will always remember Starship and the other Misfits of channel 10.

When I reminisce about CB radio, it is with nostalgia. I have memories of something that doesn't exist anymore. The southern drawl and the specialized lingo did not appeal to me. I was interested in getting closer to the core of people and looking at their differences not adding more layers of distance and making everybody sound the same. The adding of artificial, meaningless, expressions that said what they didn't mean, left me cold. So don't be calling me "good buddy," unless you mean it! 73 and hope to talk to you again sometime!

PS Starship, if you are reading this, I told you I would write this book someday! I win the bet! Just one other thing, "LAST WORD!"

Figures

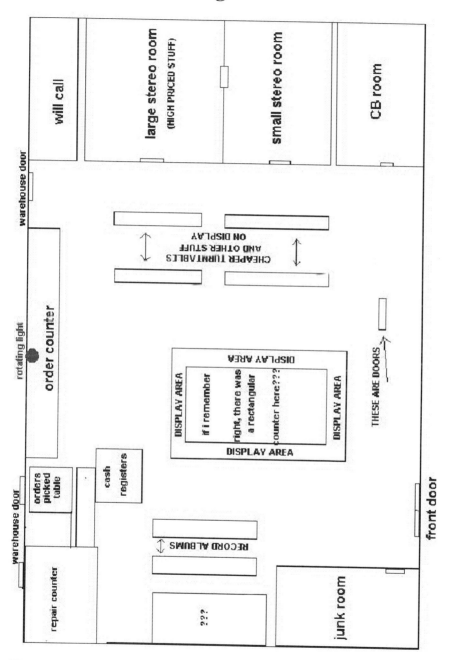

Figure 1 LRE Syosset Floor Plan

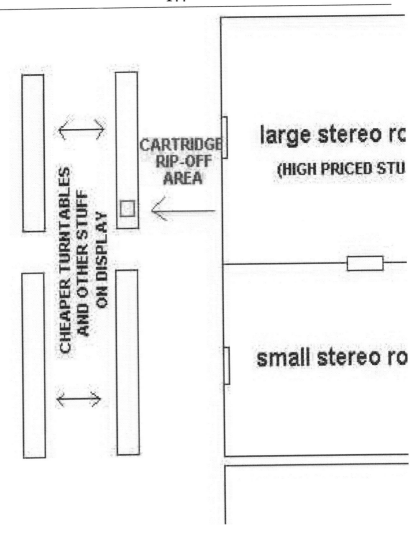

Figure 2 LRE Syosset Cartridge Rip-off Area

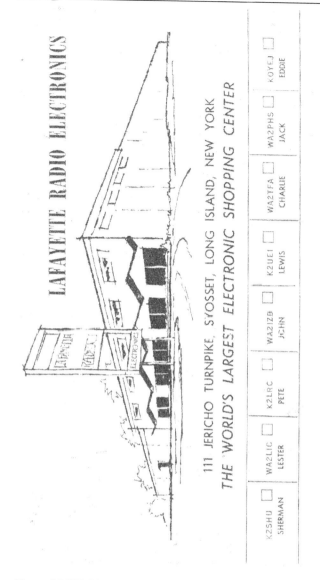

Figure 3 LRE QSL Card

Figure 4 Stink Bombs

Figure 5 Some of LRE's seasonal catalogs

Figure 6 The "Turk Kunutsie" Poster. The "Cause of Pollution" part was cutoff from the only remaining poster in existence.

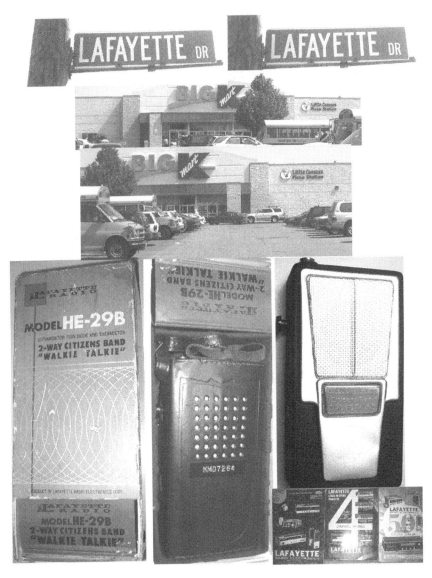

Figure 7 Memories of Lafayette Radio Electronics Corp. (LRE.) The Lafayette Drive sign – The original street sign that indicates the name of the side street that the LRE, Syosset warehouse was on. Big K-mart is the building that now occupies the former location of the Syosset LRE warehouse. The HE-29B This was my first LRE walkie-talkie that I still own. The last photo is of three yearly, LRE catalogs, including the 50th "Golden Jubilee" catalog.

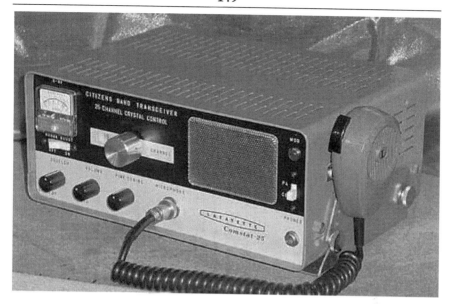

Figure 8 Comstat-25

Figure 9 HB-444-25A

Figure 10 SWR & Power

Figure 11 – SSB-140

Figure 12 – SSB-50

Figure 13 –Dynacoms

Figure 14 _ HB-525D

Figure 15 _ HB-525D

Figure 16 HB-506 - Photos courtesy of Starship

Comments?

Comments, Constructive feedback, and any additional information on the original Lafayette Radio Electronic Corp. (LRE) is encouraged and gratefully accepted.

I am still looking for taped conversations, photographs of Lafayette Radio equipment, stores, advertising giveaways, and personnel.

Any items that I use in the next version of this book or any sequel book will have credit given to the originator of the items.

My website, where I can provide autographed copies, and additional freebees (if the book is purchased here) is: http://robertzito.tripod.com/

My publisher's website is http://www.lulu.com/writer

This book can be previewed or ordered in soft cover. I also would appreciate some good reviews and feedback.

You can contact me by sending e-mail to me at:

bob-zito@comcast.net

Thanks!

Bob

About the Author

Robert J. Zito grew up In Long Island, New York. He lived first in Hicksville then moved to Syosset when he was five years old. He moved back to Hicksville where he commuted to New Jersey for 3-1/2 years. He attended Baylis elementary, Harry B. Thompson Jr. High and then Syosset High School. He went to The State University at Farmingdale and then the New York Institute of Technology at Old Westbury where he received his BSEE.

Bob is an Electrical Engineer by day and a creative writer by night. He has had three short stories published in Writer's magazines. He took first prize in the Rest Stop Writer's Creative writing contest. His articles on creative writing and writer's "flow" have been published in and are on record at the Canadian National Library.

One of his articles on writing was re-printed in the "Romance Writers of America" newsletter. He is the moderator for the "Writer's Life" on "WBBS," one of the largest writers websites on the Internet.

Bob enjoys imaginative, creative writing, writing about the creative writing process, and psychology. He writes from his gut about feelings, nostalgia, science fiction, "Coming-of-Age," and the unusual, weird things that happen to normal and sometimes supernormal people.

Bob presently resides in Redmond Washington with his lovely wife Maureen and five adult children who have flown the nest and are pursuing life in their own unique ways.